soulfire

soulfire

the birth of wild aliveness

brigitte secard

JODERE
GROUP   san diego, california

JODERE
GROUP

Jodere Group, Inc.
P.O. Box 910147
San Diego, CA 92191-0147
800.569.1002
www.jodere.com

Book design by Jennifer Ramsey
Cover design by Charles McStravick
Editorial supervision by Chad Edwards

The intent of the author is only to offer information of a general nature to help you in your quest for emotional and spiritual well-being. In the event you use any of the information in this book for yourself, which is your constitutional right, the author and the publisher assume no responsibility for your actions.

CIP data available from the Library of Congress

ISBN 1-58872-078-0

06 05 04 03   4 3 2 1
First printing, July 2003
Printed in the United States of America

a technical note to the reader from the author:

you may notice that this book has not been written in the conventional format by its use of structure, type font, color, and the absence of capital letters. this was not done on whimsy but with a precise scientific intent: to encourage neurological bilateralization. when the right brain is activated (as it is in this format), our brains are far more engaged in our ability to receive and integrate information than through the means of (traditional) primary left brain linear interpretation alone. you will also note that word usage has been done so in a way consistent with the purpose of this book: to reveal the truth contained within the meaning, in this case, of the written word. for example: beautyfull. and, some of the quotes used from ages past have been translated into a modern context (example: mankind to humankind). i have taken this liberty not only to honor the original spirit in which they were written, but also to evolve them into the language of the future which is the spirit of this book: universal inclusion.

it is my hope that you will experience and understand: *soulfire* is meant to inspire, through the expression of the written word, a new language for living. injoy!

acknowledgments

and in the beginning ...
there was gratitude.

i dedicate this book to you, mi corazon.
you are the gift that exploded my heart and opened my eyes to destiny ...
to love and be loved by you is the joy of my life. you have shown me devotion and faith like
i have never seen in human form and smithereened my lone-wolf-self poof be gone.
(and i am still giddy.) thank you for standing by me as we walk through this world
to spread love together.

i give thanks to my own soul: i am so in awe that it is my life you chose to be lived through.
you guide me, you move me-inspire me-light the fire in me ...
u r me and u return me to the
beauty of the all that is
eternally
and i can do nothing more but ssssing with a heart full of joy and wild aliveness ...
blissed be and yiippeee

my gratitude infinite belongs to the many teachers, guides, spirits, ancestors,
and friends i have been blessed with along my own journey from all over this world ...
and from beyond it.
you are with me in my every moment.
i would like to especially acknowledge the brilliant work of
flo aeveia magdalena and the impact she has had upon my life and its purpose.

to my extraordinary clients: wow. i am speechless by the beauty and transformation
i have witnessed over and over. you bring soulfire to life, and each time i am stunned
by the sheer miracle of it all. you are living proof that the greatest ecstasy is found in being
of service to the awakening of a soul. i am forever humbled by our connection.
thank you so much for allowing me to do such powerful work with you
and still remain un-guru-fied. the glory is in finding out yours.

to all those who have had the courage and conviction to stand with me and beside me in support
of bringing this work to the world against all odds + while everyone else said i was crazy — thank u
especially to stephanie, ¡yo!, brad, christine b, belinda, gary, svet — this movement was born solely
through your support. i am so grateful to paula klein for designing a work of art and for her
passionate tenacity. g / r, pauly, tom, alex, jasper, doug, chazz, nina, bullet, tate, koji,
studio 56, the knitting factory, all those precious kids who shined that night, guy, nathan,
opn-k, adge, kute, and countless more: we are indeed one circle of souls. i celebrate the presence
of each of you upon this earth and i humbly receive and give to the greatness that is u. rory rogers:
you rule, man, and yvonne, you are a goddess. to pete + glenn . . . you have been home in so many
more ways than one. and to eden, you were shown to me and you appeared when i needed
you most. my heart is so happy that you (and your beautyfull family) exist.

thank you to elixir in west hollywood. jeff stein: your support was invaluable.
my gratitude x 3.14+ to you for understanding so clearly this revolutionary vision of soulfire.
elixir is where it all began. and, ray, you are sunshine to me. i am so proud of you.

to the esteemed reverend james lawson, jr., who said "yes" and spoke on the night of the book launch. thank you, thank you, thank you for that honor. please know the courage it took to speak to you that saturday morning was the day i truly found my voice . . .

to bill maher: aren't you glad that i left working for you so i could do that "do-good" work? my gratitude to you and sheila griffiths for the opportunity to be intellectually stimulated at a job that re-ignited my passion for the political. m-d: thank u for being u.

to the many amazing musicians i have worked with who pour their hearts into the music . . . u r truth. + to all the music industry people who thought i was speaking another language . . . i was and it was this.

to all the varying spiritual groups i have worked / volunteered for . . . you were the catalyst(s) who exploded the doors open to my soul blaaazing on fire(!) i was blind but now i see . . . such amazing grace indeed. (you all inspired stage three.) a profound thank you to my alarm clock, dena. you were a wake up call to the gifts of my own soul . . . and to the true meaning of compassion. you are forever a part of my heart. (josh and sergio — you had it way back then! + the invaluable gina cloud: the world is neeeding you!!)

there is no power greater than love. and when you combine it with the manifestation of one's soul . . .
you get a force to be reckoned with. thank you to my own personal force field of genius:
dharma teamworks = the dynamic duo arielle + brian, and the fabu heidi & kat (who manifested me —
you are such the wow — smile.) chad edwards, you are truly an editor who is a dream come true
to work with. i randomly erupt into fits of joy because of your supafly-ness and brilliance.
and to the love supreme vision holder debbie luican of jodere: there is no one else i would rather
be sent than you. get ready . . . we are here to shake things up and do great things together!

to the entire jodere team: **i am honored that we represent each other.**
quite simply: you people rock the house.

and to the people who have taught me the utmost about acceptance, compassion, and
freedom . . . my own family. mom-nancy, all that i am is because of who you are. dad-fred,
you have taught me the meaning of love. i am so grateful. and, jill: you are the gift to each of us
that to be and to live one's truth is the greatest achievement in all the world.

to my soul familia → my sister meri, angel-chicken head ss, nae, steen, anna, mel+danny, nina, teri,
momo, fred peoples, bob k, demi, jj, miss zaki, vincent, k-s, vera, my bro a-thompson, ak, lu, irie, k+t, jess,
donnie, birdland and moondance books, mr. carlson, chris davis, adam, taylor, angela t, mrs. seward, and
mama wills + the entire wills family . . . you have shown me the truth of what a family is = pure love.

a special thank you to my amazing teachers don moehnke and jerry bronder . . .
and to all my political theory / philosophy / anthropology / sociology professors
whose offices i would never leave. may you now know why.

and lastly but not leastly to all of you reading this . . . know that this is the beginning of something
so magical and exciting for both of us!! we will look back at this time and smile . . . shoot —
i already am grinning like a fool. how deeply grateful i am to be experiencing this with you . . .
for we are truly one.
let us remember this and go forth to celebrate love together.
the world is waiting for what we came to give . . .
love infinite = allways,
b

soulfire
the birth of wild aliveness

intro: welcome to the dawn

at midnight on the eve of the fourth of july, 2001, this book was born.
and as it was being created, it was also shown to me the tragic events of the
months to come and the urgency in which this work was to be forwarded.

we stand now between two worlds: one that is dying, and one that is being born.
in order to enter this new world and release the other —
we need not more weapons of destruction, but instead, tools of creation.
indeed, the fate of our future and planet depends upon it.

this book is dedicated to this purpose: to begin a revolution more powerful
than any other seen before in the history of human civilization . . .

a revolution of love in action.
and from this, a new world shall truly be born.

---

someday, after we have mastered the winds, the waves, the tides, and gravity,
we shall harness for creation the energies of love. then, for the second time
in the history of the world, humankind will have discovered fire.

>> teilhard de chardin

♦   ♦   ♦   ♦

the journey you are about to begin is one that many others have taken before you . . . the only difference is that for others it occurred on mountaintops, rainy beaches, in fields, monasteries, atop ferris wheels and in recording studios . . . and all with me right next to them. i have worked with men and women of all faiths, ages, and ethnicities: from priests and psychotherapists to sex addicts, singers, and corporate executives. and every one of them has shared the same quality as you do in this moment: a passion and a willingness to connect to the purpose their soul was born for and to reside there for the rest of their lives . . . **to live the fire of their soul.** it is in this place that the greatest spiritual teacher of all time dwells . . . i am only here to introduce you and then watch you take to the sky in illumined flight.

it is your time. and so, this book has found you.

imagine this: you have been airlifted to a remote and undiscovered wild island. the only provision you are given is a map to a sacred temple. you must find this temple and face the dragons surrounding it. you have only one weapon → a magic sword. your objective is to find and enter the temple and locate within it your secret door to transport you home. the only other assistance you have is a native of this island who has been sent to you to assist in navigation, steady your course, (+ keep you amused), and most importantly . . . to be your guide on this journey.

the adventurer = you
the temple = your soul
the dragons = your disconnection from your soul
magic sword = the fire of your soul
your tour guide = me

this is the adventure of a lifetime.

it is the adventure of the awakening and the birth of your very soul. and like the successive stages of a nine month pregnancy, your adventure will come to term as you open to it. these days, about the only time most people are conscious of what it is to have a soul within a body is when they are observing a woman who is pregnant . . . when actually in truth, we are all pregnant with our own soul. this is where i come in. the best way i know how to describe my role is as your spiritual midwife. (yes, both contractions and ecstasy can be expected here, too. the process is the same, and the metaphor is truly universal.) i assist people in transforming their relationship with themselves from the most powerful place that exists — by midwifing the birth of their own soul.

every human being has a soul. and every soul has a purpose. (so, why is our world so disconnected from this truth, you say? — well, hold on there, o astute one. you are jumping ahead.) before we go any further, let us clarify one thing for the record $\rightarrow$ this process is not about goal setting, or getting over your "issues," or about how successful you are. **it is about how alive you are** . . . just ask anyone who is at the end of their life, and they will tell you that this is the ultimate success.

so, how do i know this process works? simply because it does. the people who have done this work radiate with an unmistakable fierceness of love, peace, power, joy, and a wiiiiild aliveness. (and, yes, they happen to be successful, too — but that is simply the by-product). ok, so how else can i guarantee you that this is the real deal? by the only way it counts: that i have lived every word of this book — often multiplied times a hundred. for truly, the most powerful place one can ever lead from is to inspire others by example. it is this commitment and a burning fire of my own soul that has allowed me, by grace and with great love, to receive this work and to bring it now to a world desperately crying out for it.

be warned; this is not self-help. rather, this is a call to awaken. **this is the birth of self-truth,** and it is indeed the voice of the next generation. self-truth is about being powerfull . . . of living the true power and groundedness that come from being connected to your own soul. your "self" does not need help. it does not need improvement or fixing. it does not need saving. it does not need to get real. it needs truth . . . for inside you a new world is being born right now . . . can you feel it? it is whispering to you in a voice that is calling you home.

i am honored and inspired by the many journeys of those i have been of service to before you, and now i am equally moved to be a part of your sacred journey. there is truly no greater privilege or beauty than this.

and so the time has come for us to be on our way. as i always say . . . "let the joy begin!"

>> there is only one great adventure, and that is inward, toward the self. <<
henry miller

self authority

open the door

what does the doorway to your journey look like? is it in a jungle? behind a waterfall?
inside a war bunker? take a moment and allow it to reveal itself to you now.
use this space to create it. as you do so, you are making visible the entrance
to a new world that awaits you and an adventure that is exclusively your own . . .
welcome. you have been expected here.

as you embark upon this time of great change in your life, you are doing so for many others as well. whether you know it or not, you are already a leader in and of your own life. there is no mistake that you were born at this time in history or that you are reading this right now. all of this has always been familiar to you. yes, the soul is like a time–release capsule, and now is your time, my friend . . . you are ready. the part of you that knows this is the reason you are here now.

in these times of great despair and confusion about the state of our world, there exists a truth that is as powerful as it is simple. it lives clearly both in science and in the natural world; yet, its basic application somehow eludes our detection. we turn on the news and are continually abhorred by the downward spiral of world events and, as always, the question is the same: "what is our world becoming? why is there so much violence? what can we do?" and so we look to our government to send off more troops to solve the world's problems, and we go back to business as usual until the next critical world event. what more can be done, right? well, not quite. quantum physics demonstrates over and over that the properties of the one are contained within the properties of the many. the macrocosm is contained in the microcosm and vice versa. to ignore this truth is to do so at our own peril, for this simple truth has now amassed epic proportions. the time has come for us to understand:

our world condition reflects our individual condition.

the personal is political. and there is no more closing our front door to it . . . for look behind you: it is knocking at your door and waiting to come in. we can feign confusion at our state of affairs no more. it is imperative that we understand this connection between the personal and the political if we are to move forward. we are compelled to expand our vision beyond our own lives and to begin a dialogue *of how our own lives are but a microcosm of the state of our world.* for, indeed, they are.

this book is a practical guide for what is possible in our own selves and at the same time, our entire world. as individuals <u>and</u> as nations, we must heal our past, receive its truth and from that, we can then create together the possibility of our futures. the unity of our world comes only from the unity within ourselves. there is no separation between the two. that is the objective of this book: to inspire unity in the soul of humanity **by awakening unity in the individual.**

throughout history, many leaders have come with variations of this same message; yet, without a practical and contemporary model of how to access and experience such a state in our everyday lives, it will continue to remain a distant theory. great leaders, such as gandhi and king, utilized the ideology of satyagraha, or "soulforce," to effect socio-political change. today, the lineage of consciousness they leave behind begs of us to take their fire and spread it like our lives depend upon it . . . for they do. *the urgency is very clear.* however, we must also include everything that has evolved since then that now demands our full attention. this is not our parents' political condition. no, this is our own to deal with, and it is a whole other animal. it requires an inclusion of everything from global terrorism to our sexual health to a pill-popping epidemic of generalized anxiety disorder to how we define media and the entertainment industry to *how we define ourselves . . .*

enter soulfire. it is a modern day application of how to bridge the worlds of the personal and political in a way that is culturally relevant, inclusive, and accessible.

where gandhi introduced the world to non-violence in the collective through 'soulforce,' soulfire brings the world a current and intimate look at how to create **non-violence in the self.** in order to stop the violence outside of us, we must stop the violence within us first.

soulfire is about ending warfare in the self and thereby eroding the need for continual warfare in the collective.

unity in the self, by soulfire definition, is an infrastructural template for self-connection. each stage in this journey will begin with an overview of the correlation between the collective and the individual. it will then focus on how this relates to your own life. everything about this process is meant to give you the skills to do, primarily, two things: 1) **to go2theroot.** we must develop the vision to see beyond the symptoms and into the core of the truth: in ourselves <u>and</u> in the world. 2) **to connect.the.dots.** it is necessary that we begin to make immediate assessments and connections between things that are happening at our dinner table and things that are happening in our international political relations. *they are connected.* and the sooner we can align things at the root . . . the sooner we will see things shift everywhere else. sound simple enough? the truth always is.

>> your freedom and mine cannot be separated. <<
nelson mandela

this book is not a treatise, a critique, or an analysis of modern society. it is not a complex examination of the state of our world. there is already an abundance of books on that subject (thank you to our many brilliant authors). this is, however, something quite different and a whole lot more in-joy-able. (see?) this is a glimpse at what can be. it is not an exploration of the problem, but instead it is the doorway to creating the solution. **soulfire** is a manifesto intended to create an entirely new possibility for the human condition . . . a possibility that the world has never before seen. and this book is your road map to creating it in your own life.

this experience is meant to be hands–on and interactive. there will often be opportunities for you to journal (in your own special soulfire journal of your design) and / or discuss the concepts after each section. that is the point. involve as many people as you want in these dialogues but make sure to keep this process your own. it requires your full integrity. this is your own "spiritual cookbook" meant for you to refer to for the rest of your life as you continue to deepen your mastery to each of the principles. like a concentric circle, living your soul is something you never stop discovering new ways to explore and experience. this is a book you will want to take with you through future years and eventually leave behind as a part of your legacy . . . it is like finding the secret decoder to a body of knowledge that has been lost for thousands of years. *it is the magic key that unlocks the vault to the secrets of living your soul.* you can search far and wide . . . and you will discover there is still no greater treasure to be found. this is the place of all beginnings and endings. and when you become what is on these pages, your life will have indeed become a revolution of love in action. you will be so wildly alive that you will find it hard to remember the first time you even read these words . . . (+ you will be too busy lighting up the world and having multiple life orgasms, anyway.) who knew revolution could be this good??? oh, just trust me, it can.

soulfire is a comprehensive one-stop-shop to awaken and inspire who you are here to be = the gift that you bring to this world = mucho wild aliveness.

there is only one rule you must remember: there is **no limit** to joy. so get crackin! i dare you to defy master p (so would he, i bet).

assignment:

a:

write a letter to your soul declaring your intention and commitment to this process. what is it you desire to experience as a result of this soulfire adventure? claim it now. sign the letter. fold it and place it in an envelope. glue the back of the envelope onto a page in your soulfire journal so that you have now created a pocket on that page.

(+ put anything else on / in this pocket that reflects your excitement to begin this: a favorite quote / a picture of an island that reminds u of the joy of your soul / a ticket stub from the movie that cracked your heart wide-open and spoke to you deeply . . . completely make it your own).

p.s. making and using a soulfire journal, by the way, is only for people who are oh-so-hot; yet, oh-so-cool all at the same time. being fascinating is a pre-req. perhaps might that apply to you? yes, i thought it would. check this: not only can revolution be joyfull, but it can be done with much style, too. got to love that.

the birth of cool is all about a soul on fire.
so, light it up.

>> because you are alive, everything is possible. <<
thich nhat hanh

b:

read over the following list, then make a list of the ten topics that seem to jump off the page and call your name.

take your time to read the entire list and notice what pulls you . . .

power	nourishment	enlightenment
love	family	commitment
soul-authority	money	spirituality
aliveness	emotions	death
self-worth	contraception	marriage
career	success	the masculine
peace	the soul	the body
self-expression	food	vulnerability
sexuality	pregnancy	trust
relationships	freedom	faith
desire	accountability	the feminine
unity	compassion	honesty
meditation	joy	truth
creativity	connection	acceptance
romance	pain	beauty
god	destiny	passion

after you have made your list of the ten that you've chosen on a separate sheet of paper, write for each one, these two things:

1) your present understanding of the concept in general.

2) your present relationship to the concept in your own life / self right now. be willing to tell the absolute truth to yourself as you write. be sure to write whatever comes to you; sentence structure is not important. try not to think about each response too much; feel into it, and respond as soon as you receive your feeling.

c:

read over what you wrote for each topic.

what do you notice about the relationship between your:

(a) external,
    and
(b) internal worlds from doing this exercise?

what is your experience of these concepts in how you apply them to other people in contrast with how you experience them within yourself?

>> as human beings, our greatness lies not so much in being able to remake the world . . .
as in being able to remake ourselves. <<

mahatma gandhi

self authority

stage one: preparing for greatness

there is a greatness waiting for you.

we are busy, we are distracted, we are cynical. but this greatness waits. through a speech by dr. king

or the story of the grinch or even a bumper sticker, this greatness finds you

in a moment, unlikely or untimely, and suddenly you find yourself connected to humanity

in a way that shocks you. and this greatness will hold you up so high and strong that

any previous version of yourself seems flimsy.

>> magazine ad for timberland boots

suggested soulfire soundtracks for this section:
<> amel larrieux: *infinite possibilities*   <> claude challe: *sun*
<> family stand: *connected*   <> bebel giberto: *tanto tempo*   <>miles davis: *the birth of cool*
<> telepopmusik: *just breathe*   <> yo yo ma: *bach / the cello suites*

suggested soulfire fieldtrip destinations for this section:
<> attend a random college graduation ceremony   <> open-mic night at a cafe
<> a park with a playground and a bunch of kids   <> watching babies breathe

everyone can be great, because everyone can serve.

you only need a heart full of grace ...

>> dr. martin luther king, jr.

busy. busy. busy. ask anyone how things in their life have been, and you will generally get the same response: "it's been so crazy lately. you know how it is. i can't believe it's the end of the week already! where does the time go? i just have so much going on . . . "

the chinese word for "busy" consists of two characters: heart and killing. stress-related illnesses have been proven to be the number one cause of death in our society. yet, toil we do, and vigilantly so in the futile pursuit of finishing that never ending list of things "to do" (not to mention our relentless drive to have). anything that hints at what we may be yearning "to be" in our life is deemed wholly impractical. but what if the actual quality of your life changed dramatically from your ability to be and to do in synergy? and that your beingness has a more direct effect on your health than any other single factor in your life?

fact: the spiritual and material dwell together as one world. we have made a monumental attempt to separate them throughout history. but, unfortunately, we have only succeeded in separating from ourselves. we have very efficiently removed the sacred from life and converted it instead to a distorted pile of errands, obligations, acquisitions, and achievements. we have lost our connection to our divine fire in being alive and the clear joy that always follows it. we have quietly and slowly, over thousands of years, lost our soul. and no amount of success, fame, beauty, or wealth will substitute. in fact, it will only make more apparent what is missing both in the individual and collective life.

our soul is urgently calling out to us, in one and in all, to come home and reconnect. there is but one way and place to do this: through our own body. the "grounded state of being" is a structure of alignment with the body and breath to fully utilize your life force and experience your full aliveness in every moment. it is the center of your power and your continual connection to yourself.

>> the glory of all creation is a human person fully alive. <<
irenaeus

15

---

to walk through this world with the innocence and wonder of a child
and
with the wisdom and centeredness of an elder
requires us to be rooted in both the physical and spiritual worlds . . .
=
we need roots and wings.

---

breath + body in synthesis
creates the doorway that brings our inner and outer worlds together.

joy is the presence of and connection to the divine in our bodies and our selves.
where there is connection to our soul, there is aliveness.
where there is aliveness, there is gratitude. where there is gratitude,
there is joy in simply being.

the grounded state of being
opens you first to the presence of joy consistently flowing in your body,
and then to the presence of joy constantly flowing in your life.

>> the most visible joy can only reveal itself to us when we've transformed it within. <<
rainer maria rilke

assignment:

a:

grounded state of being	vs.	**frantic state of doing**

(the oak tree)	**(the piece of paper)**
> connected to the divine life force	> disconnected / phone off the hook(!)
> unlimited in what you can give and receive	> limited everything
> powerfull	> powerless
> free / pro-active	> reactive and highly stressed out
> strong	> blown over by any old breeze
> centered and totally o p e n	> energy trapped above the neck
> deep breathing	> shallow rapid breathing
> resonant voice	> nasal / throaty speaking tone
> posture aligned	> hunched forward / low back collapsed / shoulders knotted

practice the grounded state of being (practice makes permanent).
also, initially you may choose to have someone read this to you until it becomes familiar:

<> stand with your feet hip distance apart;
   feet perfectly parallel (big toe and heel in line);
   toes spread and suction-cupped to the ground;
   ankles flexible and knees unlocked;
<> hips open and warmed up like a hula hooper.

>> not all speed is movement. <<
toni cade bambara

17

<> spine straight and low back in line with upper back (stand against a wall and slide down to a seated position; knees bent at 90 degrees to practice this aspect of aligning your spine — pressing your lower back into the wall); abdomen is the backbone of your heart = long and strong;

<> shoulders roll back and heart comes forward; chin over heart, head relaxed, feel your jaw drop / soften;

<> shoulders over hips and hips over ankles; roll your head slowly in circles in each direction, feeling your head and neck relax and release.

<> feels like you are being pulled into the sky by puppet strings — while at the same time being deeply rooted in the earth.

breath comes from under your bellybutton and under your ribs.
(just like babies breathe)

isolate the chest to be still as you breathe. try this: lie down on your back → put a big book over your belly button. breathe into your core and feel your stomach fill out with air as the book rises and your rib cage and middle back expand out. then as slowly as you can, exhale and feel everything gently collapse back down. continue this slow and deep breath pattern. find the instinctual ocean-like rhythm of your own breath. **to breathe in this way is to immediately connect to your soul.** this factor alone is enough to change your life forever. know this: *do not underestimate this way of breathing*. it is the secret of the ages and wisdom of sages. it is the difference between making a choice clearly and serenely, or having an anxiety attack. your life literally hangs on your every breath.

what are the similarities between the way you breathe-stand-speak and the way you live?
spend time observing the state of your self and those around you.
what do you observe?

your state creates your life.

>> what you cannot find in your own body, you will not find elsewhere. <<
the upanishads

happiness and joy are not one in the same.
happiness is the elation that accompanies good fortune,
while joy is the evidence of the divine presence in the human experience.
joy is not a destination; it is a way of traveling.
>> mary manin morrissey

---

b:
when do you feel most connected to your own joy?

write a poem
about your own brand of joy in your **soulfire** journal.

~ feel free to use colors ~

---

fact: our spirituality is meant to be joyfull, not high drama and hard labor. really.

>> joy is deeper than sorrow because joy seeks eternity. <<
friedrich nietzsche

for journaling . . . go2theroot: what is your in-joy-ability?

known → the amount of joy you can experience in your lifetime is infinite.
so, on a 1 to 10 scale, how much joy is presently in your world right now?
+ looking at how you are currently living your life,
how alive do you actually feel in it?
(and . . . how is that working out for you?)
if we know joy is an internal state = that you bring the joy with you wherever you go,
(think byoj), then where is your joy being held hostage in your life
and by whom / what is it being held? how could you liberate your joy today?
what would it take for you to *bring the joy*
instead of eternally waiting for it to show up . . . ?
list some ways for **joy creation** in your daily life.
what role does gratitude play?
cap it off by drawing a picture in your soulfire journal
of what you look like living joyfully.

this is all muy importante: for the absence of joy leads to tragic ends. see below.

connect.the.dots . . . joy is not a luxury. it is a political necessity:
how is an absence of joy linked to how people interact with each other in your community
on a practical level? how is "the grounded state of being" related to, say, safe driving
(shallow breathing and being highly reactive = road rage). now, how about this:
how is the lack of people living in the grounded state create our current epidemic
of **frenzied reactivity** and violence everywhere in the world?

consider this story:

once, a young woman asked the 14th century poet hafiz this question:

"what is the sign that someone has connected to the divine in themselves?"

his response: "dear, they have dropped the knife. they have dropped the cruel knife

most often used upon their own tender self and others."

tell me:

what is it that you hold in your hand?

know that your hands are the hands of the world.

21

self authority

stage two: planting the seed — remembering

love
is the law
of our
being.

>> mahatma gandhi

suggested soulfire soundtracks for this section:
<> john coltrane: *a love supreme*(!)   <> sarah mclachlan: *surfacing*
<> sade: *love deluxe*   <> joe sample + lalah hathaway: *the song lives on*
<> miriam makeba: *homeland*   <> john lennon: *imagine*

suggested soulfire fieldtrip destinations for this section:
<> museum with neolithic / paleolithic exhibits   <> a monastery
<> invite friends over and watch *the matrix*. twice. then discuss.
<> sitting on the playground swings under a full moon   <> the beach

it is difficult to remember a time when colonialism, imperialism, wars, and genocides did not permeate our past. can you remember a time when power was not equated with violence and destruction, and life was about more than just getting through it . . . ? where fear did not dominate our every move? these times did exist, thankfully. there is ample archaeological documentation that confirms it wasn't always like this. (our gratitude to the work of marija gimbutas, leonard shlain, riane eisler, et al.) even if you have studied intimately such a time in history, it seems likely very distant now, almost as if it could have never even happened. today, war footage is wedged in between shampoo commercials and the latest sitcom promo while our kids practice killing people on video games. we build our walls higher and higher around our houses while moving farther away from our neighbors. technology has given us a myriad of ways to almost reach someone (whom we don't really want to talk to anyway), leaving them a voice mail as we step over the homeless person on the street, all while busily rushing to see the latest hollywood it-girl(?) movie. road rage violence is now as common as traffic. we buy more guns than we do books and build more prisons than schools. we are constantly ready for the next attack — whether from our co-worker, wife, or the country across the ocean . . . and on and on the list goes. where can all this fear possibly originate? if love is truly the most powerful and alchemical force in the universe, why then is it not utilized to transmute the rampant darkness in our world? why is it not used to dissolve the shackles of prejudice and hatred that seem to lie across the earth in these times we live in? where is the peace? *where is the love*?

if love could speak to us, it would probably say this:

"i have waited for you for such a long time . . .
when will you at last greet me in your own heart?"

>> the reason why the world lacks unity, and lies broken and in heaps, is because man is disunited within himself. <<
ralph waldo emerson

the degree we are disconnected from seeing the presence of love in each other is truly the degree in which we are disconnected from seeing it in ourselves. this alienation and distrust of others is but the shadow cast from our own hearts.

thomas merton had been known to exclaim: "there is no way of telling people that they are all walking around shining like the sun . . . there are no strangers! if only we could see each other as we really are all the time, there would be no more war and hatred." however, *unless we can learn to see the truth in ourselves, we will surely never see the truth in each other*. and yet to know the truth in ourselves, we must know where to look. we must know where to begin . . .

wondrously, there is an immediate anecdote to fear and disconnection from our own soul: it is the ripple in the pond of the world and it is called "the daily art of self-connection and the creation of sacred space." many would have you believe this entails austere and terribly complicated guidelines. it does not. meditation and self-connection are as natural as falling asleep. those who tell you otherwise you can thank. and keep on walking. you are, however, required to create it as your very own space of rest, release, nourishment, guidance, expression, inspiration, and (of course) joy. this is your doorway to the true self and the only way the world is truly changed . . . one person at a time.

spirituality is not about getting away from the world; it is about entering it more deeply and truth-fully. your daily meditation / self-connection is not something you get out of the way in the morning and then run out the door to cuss at the taxi driver blocking your car. it is something that eventually will inform your entire day and life and perhaps in the near future, our world.

there is an immense power in the remembering of truth all day long.

>> there is only one way in which one can endure people's inhumanity to other people and that is to try, in one's own life, to exemplify people's humanity to other people. <<

alan paton

simply start in a corner of your home with a small sacred space where you practice your self-connection, and then eventually, the entire world will become your altar. soon, everywhere becomes an opportunity for self-connection and in time you will find that feeling continually grounded and connected to yourself will be as natural as breathing. for it will be. and the irony is we think our regular frantic-pace way of living is more productive. hardly. self-connection is supremely practical. you will be stronger and more effective than ever before, and there will be an unmistakable ease and flow to your life.

this is true power, for you will know it when you feel it.

>> he who gains victory over others is strong; but he who gains victory within himself is all powerful. <<

lao-tzu

on the art of creating sacred space <> rule numero uno: there isn't any. here are some ideas to get you started: write your own gratitude prayer / stretch / play music / light candles / set a timer so you don't have to watch the clock / sit in silence and listen to the voice of your soul (fyi: it is speaking to you all the time) / paint + draw + color / in the morning, set an intention for your day / at night, reflect upon the meaning of all that occurred / connect to your breath / place one hand on your heart. breathe. ask it what it needs right now / put up pictures of your kids or pictures of when you were one / hold an object that has deep meaning / cry if you need to / laugh if you want to / journal / sing yourself a lullaby / read aloud from a sacred text / go outside and witness the wisdom of all of life inside a tree / look at a butterfly and see your own self within it . . . notice the ease in which it flies. (hint)

the only necessity in the creation of your daily sacred space and self-connection is that you commit to it and that it be uninterruptible(!!) as it is done *daily* → approximately 10–30ish minutes every day. (when is the right time for you?) this is key! keep your word to you = this is a place where magic and miracles occur. if you attend to this time with the utmost humility and reverence, your soul (a.k.a. the root of love) will begin to speak in a voice and with a presence that you will know as none other.

and often, an experience of peace, ecstasy, and urgency combined will seize you . . . simply be still, and be patient. (fyi: the soul does not respond to demands, or petulance, or probing lights.)

i am sitting on a mountain.
i am casting shadows into the sky.
i did not invite it but the sun has come
and is now playing tag with my feet . . .
where do you think you will be when the divine reveals itself inside of you?

>> hafiz

---

it is the ability to determine the truth for oneself that distinguishes man from brute. to find truth completely is to realize oneself and one's destiny.

>> mahatma gandhi

---

clarity on spiritual definitions often confused:

"true self"	"false self"
=	=
connected to soul	**disconnected from soul**

> love	> fear
> truth	> distrust
> purity	> shame / judgment
> life as creation	> life as survival
> the root of destiny	> the root of misery
> the expression of one's humanity	> the expression of one's inhumanity
> peaceful	> violent in word or deed
> aliveness	> numbness-deadness

> **power as internal —**
  cannot be given or taken away

> **power as external —**
  is given to you and taken away by others

>> the one thing in the world, of value, is the active soul. <<
ralph waldo emerson

self-truth 101

~ to live your soul is to be wildly alive ~

a common q: how does one know when they are connected to their soul?
the answer is simply that you just know. consider — how do you know you love your mother?
how do you know you want to marry someone? you just feel it and you know. it is nothing
to be analyzed, and you could not even talk yourself out of it if you tried. words cannot explain it . . .
it just is. what are the most profound and real experiences in life? they are the things that we feel.
so why not have the things that we feel be the truth within our soul which brings us profound levels
of aliveness instead of what is commonly known as the 'normal life' replete with the daily array of
numbness, stress, alienation and anxiety? (here is where i do the soulfire dance of joy
because aliveness is my daily real-ity. and i believe it can be the world's, too.)

being connected to yourself is to be in a state of clarity, joy, and peace
regardless of what is going on around you =
a peace that passeth understanding, as they say.

self-connection is about finding and trusting the truth within you . . .
which then creates the doorway to manifesting it all around you.

>> you need not do anything . . . remain sitting at your table and listen, you need not even listen, just wait
and you need not even wait . . . just become quiet, and still, and solitary, and the world will offer itself
to you to be unmasked; it has no choice. it will roll in ecstasy at your feet. <<

franz kafka

enlightenment:
is nothing you have to do or "get to" by torturing yourself because someone wearing white said so . . .
it is the access, recognition, <u>and</u> expression of the truth of your own soul (a.k.a. unreasonable joy).
it occurs outside of space and time. + does not happen through the intellect but through the heart.
note: there is no such thing as spiritual superiority. the "e" word is oft abused by those who act as if
they are holier than thou. (whom we shall fondly call *guru-divas*). those who are truly illumined are
always exceedingly humble and see greatness in everyone, not just themselves. (wow! imagine that!?)

destiny:
the experience of the essence of your soul from moment to moment.
the future is created from this state as you live it. not something to do but to be.

destiny / enlightenment = being fully connected in the now. (extreeeme aliveness)

whatever beauty you see here and there is only a projection of your own being. whenever
you have felt a sense of great beauty, that is when you have been in touch with yourself.
because you are so, so beautiful. that is why something else in the world also looks beautiful
to you. you get a glimpse of self. a little shower from this glimpse comes to you. when waves
of beauty come to you unceasingly, that is called enlightenment. >> sri sri ravi shankar

bliss = the ability to find and experience the truth wherever you go.
(kind of like an existential game of *where's waldo*)

>> everything has beauty, but not everyone sees it. <<
confucius

to have faith in yourself, you must first know the beauty of your own heart

assignment:

a:
. . . to know the beauty of your own heart, you must first, what? yep. connect to it. pick your sacred space for daily self-connection in your environment and begin its creation. **today.**

b:
make a list of all the love present in your life — then celebrate those people. !wildly! throw them a party, decorate their front doors, or just savor it quietly at home on a friday night with a glass of wine as a party of one. (bonus points: did you include yourself?)

for journaling:
what does it look like and feel like to live in each of your two possible states of being: your **connected** self or your **disconnected** self? at the top of a blank page, list two columns = one for each expression of self. on the left side, write 'my disconnected self,' and on the top of the right side, 'my connected self.' draw a line down the center of the page. now, describe your daily life in both columns. get very specific so that you can clearly discern one side from the other. (compare and contrast your breathing, how you feel, look, the way you dress, eat, walk, communicate, drive, socially interact, etc. in each state of being.) + fyi, there is no such thing as being in both at the same time. it is either one or the other. ahem, chances are that the first time you do this, the most detailed and extensive side of the page will likely be the side that starts with the letter "d." (just so you know.) we do not have a whole heckuva lot of examples in self-connection walking around in the world, so don't feel bad.

think first monkey in space = us. we are blazing a new way. so sit back and enjoy.
you are indiana jones for the soul.

connect.the.dots. "the truth is out there" (because, really, it is. you will know when you find it because it will match with the truth that is *in here* = in you).

look at how the history of human civilization has been told only in fragments. (get on the 'net and start researching everything from columbus day to how the consciousness of cave people is not fully indicative of all of our human ancestors to how the most ancient theological systems were centered around a universal divine being that was by no means male. go on and check it.)

how are understanding and honoring the truth of our collective past related to unlocking the truth of our future as a world? . . . now look at this same concept i*n your own life*. we will revisit this theme as it is a pivotal aspect of this journey.

>> you know quite well, deep within you, that there is only a single magic, a single power, a single salvation . . . and that is called loving. <<   herman hesse

self authority

stage three: the conception — connecting

…be your own
teacher
and your own
disciple.

>> jiddu krishnamurti

suggested soulfire soundtracks for this section:
<> rachelle ferrell: *individuality* (can i be me?)   <> ani difranco: *revelling reckoning*
<> radiohead: *amnesiac*   <> dianne reeves: *in the moment: live*
<> *finding forrester*: watch movie and listen to soundtrack. repeat as needed.

suggested soulfire fieldtrip destinations for this section:
<> take a one day road-trip somewhere you have never been and meet folks
<> go to a concert by yourself   <> sit on the edge of a pier at sunset

know the golden rule?

of course, you do. everyone knows the golden rule. however, part of this work, as it was given to me, was to give to you the truth about the golden rule, and . . . well, the emperor is naked. our golden rule is missing one critical step — how do you do unto someone else if you are confused about how to do unto (love / honor) your own self? how can you teach someone else how to love you if you don't know how or **the who in you** to love?

see, it somehow never explained that minor detail. and, as a result, millions of people have been doing unto others in every kind of dysfunctional way and then getting mad when they are the recipient of someone else's confusion, expectations, and unmet projected needs.

in this time of psychoanalytic genius, gifted healers, leaders of consciousness, and brilliant gurus — you would think that someone would be able to successfully articulate a way of how to answer this question for oneself. unfortunately, there is a proliferating breed of those who are more interested in being the guru as they issue forth oracles answering your questions for you about who you are and your illustrious destiny (which usually, by the way, has something to do with them), while their followers sit in rapt attention at their feet being fed <> than those who would rather teach someone how to fish and how to actually answer these questions for themselves. (oh, and risk losing all their followers because they would be too busy following their own lives instead of following the life of their deified answer-man / woman.) *the greatest teachers in history are those who render themselves obsolete by guiding us to answer our own questions ourselves.* (yes, friends, even if it puts them out of a job and the spotlight.) fact: it is a delusion of power for anyone to tell you who you are. and a serious one at that. every human being must eventually answer that question for, and from, their own soul. **welcome to self-truth.**

there is greatness and ordinariness in every human being and this applies equally to all "gurus" and their followers . . . for there is only one guru in all of the world: **your own soul.**

>> the greatest good you can do for another is not just to share your riches, but to reveal to them their own. <<
benjamin disraeli

this is why some of self-help and its many facilitators are quite often,
despite their best intentions, useless at the end of the day. self-help frequently
enslaves you to keep coming back for more while it simultaneously claims it is liberating you.
the litmus test? the pressure to keep coming back. and, please, bring two friends.
it actually enforces the very thing it claims to free you of: shame and dependency.
all of your issues / wounds / problems better get "cleaned up" or you are surely doomed.
(or did you forget that you are already skilled enough at beating yourself into submission?)
enough already!! have we not had our fill of self-improvement as being a dominatrix for the soul?
cripes! enough growth by pain!! can someone grow by joy pleeease?? contrary to popular belief,
life is not *earth school*. we are not here to sweat out earning gold stars for being good little
children and learning our lessons. in truth, human existence is far closer to the idea of recess.
say it with me now: *i am here to know joy*. that is our original state friends. and you knew it
before our modern world of disconnection systematically stripped it out of you.
this is the true innocence of childhood, and, yes, of life.
the joy of aliveness is natural.
connect to your soul, and you will find this truth out for yourself.
that is the point of self-authority. don't take it from me . . .
take it from the only person who knows the truth: <u>you</u>.

self-help is the boat that has carried us across the river.
yes, we do have much to thank it for . . . but we are in new times now, and a boat
is not going to carry us up this mountain. it is time for a new way.
(and we can be grateful and revolutionary in the same breath.)
it is time for the next . . .

transformation is not, i repeat, not, boot camp.
hear ye, hear ye → you don't need a guru . . . you need yourself.
enter self-authority.
in the word "authority," the root "authos" in greek = self.
hallelujah at last!

---

objective of self-authority:
to have a connection to your soul as unshakable
as your sense of existence this moment

---

self-authority, a.k.a. soul–authority, is the singular most powerful way to illuminate your life.
it immediately removes you from the land of patheticism ("why can't i ever get it right?
why won't he tell me i'm beautiful? why won't she commit?") and catapults you
into a place of clarity, wisdom, and power.

you cannot love yourself by substitution = loving someone else and then hoping
and praying they will love you back.

nope, no one else will do but you. when you understand this in your heart —
the world will open to you.
apply this and be prepared for a love flood.

>> don't accept that others know you better than you know yourself. <<
sonja friedman

the law of self-precedence:

how you understand, value, and see yourself is the precedent
for how the world sees, values, and understands you.

what you give to yourself, you can give to others
what you do not give to yourself, you cannot give to others.

what you receive from yourself, you can receive from others
what you do not receive from yourself, you cannot receive from others.

(now read it all again, slowly)

using this is like having x-ray vision while observing the princess and the pea. we spend most of our lives tossing and turning — changing partners, jobs, and moving around the world — never finding the root of what wakes us up in the night.

right now, think of any relationship where you are frustrated. now ask yourself — am i giving to myself what i am demanding from them? hmmmmm. until the answer is yes, it would be wise to stop harassing that person. *do not ask from others what you are not willing to do yourself.* it is not them you are frustrated with. it is <u>you</u>. there is something that wants to be heard and honored in you.

note: this is also the reason why unconditional love is very rarely seen in the human condition. simply apply the law of self-precedence = you must be giving it to yourself before you endeavor to give it to another. self-truth: unconditional love is real and possible. it is just that very, very few, until now, have understood how to connect to it in their own self in order to be able to express it to another. to experience unconditional love in another, you must first find its source = **your own soul.**

>> you've got to find the force inside you. <<
joseph campbell

known: you cannot give others a script of how to love you — your choice is this: either receive it, accept it, or reject it, but you can never control (try as you might) how another human being loves you. how you experience their love only reflects how you experience the love within yourself. without this wisdom, you will endlessly try to fix the mirror, not knowing you are actually the source of its reflection. it is time to stop ex-pecting and start in-specting. (we will continue to deepen the concept of the mirror later.)

how the law of self-precedence translates in daily life:

---

when i honor myself, my self expression will honor me.

---

example: "when i do my daily self-connection, i am able to communicate clearly with my wife, and i find myself so overcome in moments by how much i love to love her and how grateful i am for her in my life. and then, of course, our sex life goes to a whole other level." (what do you now think the value of daily self-connection is?)

true wisdom lives in self-discovery.
(example: explain to me about the last really great self-help book you read. now, explain to me what you learned when you first lived on your own . . .)

your heart is never confused. never.
the only thing that is unclear is our ability to hear it.
the word *hear* is in the center of our heart.
(example: are you in love right now?)

>> there is no mistaking love. you feel it in your heart. it is the common fiber of life, the flame of that heats our soul, energizes our spirit and supplies passion to our lives. it is our connection. <<

elisabeth kübler-ross

there is really only one choice we ever make in life:
to be who you truly are or to be someone else's idea of who you are.
which choice does your life reflect? (example: whose job do you really have?)

being true to yourself
is the
one and only
yurok indian
law.

>> which can say more than this rich praise, that you alone are you. <<
william shakespeare

+ clarity by distinction:

self-worth =
my value on who i am underneath my gender, personality, appearance, talents, etc. the divine presence within the "who" at the heart of you — it is the expression of your spirit.

it is what is left when everything else falls away. it is allways the truth that remains.

self-esteem =
my value on what i do. my roles, talents, skills i utilize to do something in the world. you can have all the self-esteem in the world and have zero self-worth. this is true about most people our world deems successful.

the singular greatest act of courage by any human being begins with this: to truly know the beauty of their own heart and to be open to the greatness and gifts of their own soul. this is not egoic narcissism or self-aggrandizement. no, this is humility of the most profound kind. it is in this place where the love and awe of one's own true self inevitably and indelibly intersect with a deep and enduring love for all humanity. **come home to your own heart and soul and you will, at last, come home and deeply connect to all the world around you.**

acknowledge yourself with a sense of gratitude for who you are every day. never forget the fact that you even exist is a divine creation and a miracle.

>> if you love all things, you will also attain the divine mystery that is in all things. for then your ability to perceive the truth will grow every day, and your mind will open itself to an all-embracing love … <<

fyodor dostoyevsky

going2theroot: for journaling / discussion:

soulfire = the greatest leaders are followers . . . of their own soul.

we have already defined that **self-truth** is about the power of being connected to our own soul.
yet, we are living in a culture where we are continually encouraged to give our power away . . .
to trust the perceptions of other people before we trust ourselves. we are searching, not for insight,
but *for the answers to our lives* in workshops, seminars, healers, success coaches, life strategists, psychics,
therapists, doctors, churches, friends, families, lovers, celebrities, political leaders, television shows,
advertising, self-help gurus . . . you name it. it seems that everyone else is the authority on who
we are **but us**. yes, i am saying we have become addicted to validation. we are like junkies constantly
looking for our next fix of approval and direction. somehow and someway, it has become normal to
silence our own selves and view power as outside of us. self-victimization has become casual and
expected. and every time we give ourselves and our power away, there are five people ready and willing
to take the goods, run, and claim it all for themselves. just picture a mrs. potato head with no arms, legs,
lips, or eyeballs trying to make her way in the world. not pretty. indeed, it is an unfortunate epidemic.
+ believe me, no one will even stop to ask why you have voluntarily abdicated your own throne,
not even if you are a "miss hottie-pants" just like uma thurman was in *hysterical blindness*.
yet, this is nor a good thing or a bad thing . . .
it is simply what we have chosen,
and has subsequently created the state of our world as we now know it today.
(and we have most definitely reached our fork in the road.)

>> if rosa parks had taken a poll before she sat down on the bus in montgomery, she'd still be standing. <<
mary frances berry

connect.the.dots:
what would it look like if we shifted from powerless to power-full?
a transformation from power outside us to power within ourselves . . .

in our world?
+
and in our own life?

how then are **self-authority** and **self-truth** revolutionary in a world where it is celebrated
to live in disconnection from the truth and power in ourselves?

>> the greatest danger in life, that of losing one's own self, may pass off quietly as if it were nothing; yet every other loss,
that of an arm, a leg, five dollars, . . . etc., is sure to be noticed. <<
søren kierkegaard

assignment:

your love bank account +
the adventure we've all been waiting for . . .

a:
apply the law of self-precedence to yourself today and ask this question:

how fiercely and freely do you love? yourself? — those in your life? — people who look different from you and live in other countries? reminder: when i connect to, love, and honor the truth of myself — i can connect to, love, and honor the truth of other people. all people. (fact: unity must precede diversity.)

soulfire = show your love. practice humanity.

b:
your most profound and fun assignment ever as we travel back to the future:
the adventure to power!

> in your journal, write the story of your life as a mythical adventure —
  a fictional yet autobiographical account.

> starting at the beginning of your life and ending with:
  a spectacular-fireworks-parade homecoming to your soul and your true self.

> you are the hero/ine!

>> i am never afraid of what i know. <<
anna sewell

> write your cast of characters: who has had the most significant influence — positive and negative. name them, starting with you (begin with your own character name).

> then list the events of your life **of greatest impact** in chronological order — events that scaled the heights of love or the depths of pain. what are the triumphs? disasters? how do they contribute to your journey and subsequent victory?

> then proceed to weave it all together and compose your story — usually no more than 3 pages.

finale!
using playdoh / finger puppets / stick people / or hey a musical score and
live actors if u can . . . act it out. it may be for you alone or an audience of one very trusted friend
that is reading this book too. if so, then you can be the audience for each other.
(as a bookclub, team soulfire is a very hip idea by the way.)
remember, you will be opening new doors as you do this,
so make sure you are discerning of who + what are around you.
some people have laughed the whole way through their own personal sci-fi adventure
while others have sobbed while holding plastic chickens.
the point is to keep going until the end of your story.

trust that something very powerful is occurring.
for it truly is . . .

[this is where the flower opens from self-authority into self-compassion]

without this next step, you could spend years and years stuck here painfully . . .
for without self-compassion, you are trapped as a victim to your own self.

and with compassion, you possess something more powerful than steel
and more valuable than gold . . . compassion is the greatest healer of them all.

now, get ready to connect some serious dots as you turn the page →

self
compassion

stage four: life forms — the awakening

until he **extends** his circle
of **compassion**
to include **all living things,**
man will not himself find peace.

>> albert schweitzer

suggested soulfire soundtracks for this section:
<> gil scott heron: *the revolution will not be televised*   <> living colour: *cult of personality*
<> oceania: *the maori voice of new zealand*   <> radiohead: *hail to the thief*
<> system of a down: *toxicity*   <> red hot chili peppers: *blood sugar sex magik*
<> me'shell ndegeocello: *cookies — the anthropological mixtape*

suggested soulfire fieldtrip destinations for this section: (in random order)
<> churches of varying religions   <> your local ghetto   <> a strip club
(hey, this is an adventure of the soul . . . i never said it would be boring.)

during ancient greece, when plato spoke that the "polis" is a spiritual place, he was speaking not only for the political institutions of his country, but he was speaking for all of the world and for all time to follow. his original intention, along with zeno, socrates, as well as many other masterminds in the art of governing whom had lived in periods even prior to his, was to create a model of spirituality-and-state that upheld the sanctity of life for all of its citizens. to philosophize on the highest good of humankind and to concern oneself with politics was the same thing . . . *back then*. the service of freedom, liberty, and justice for one was synonymous with serving the highest good of the all.

throughout history, we have ardently devoted ourselves to pursuing a worldview and political ideology that originally began as a synthesis of spirituality-and-state; over time, however, it gradually morphed into the merging of church-and-state. then, in recent centuries, a pervasive cultural marriage of the objectives of religion-and-state have evolved. the ideals of what i am calling this spirituality + state model have been slowly inverted into what we now see today: a political body influenced far more by economics and religious socio-political agendas than it has been by the commitment to promoting unity in humankind. in fact, this model actually promotes the opposite: it generates hatred and division. as a result, we have seen tyranny, slavery, and oppression rip apart country after country in a vicious cycle over and over . . . and often done so under the name of the same presence invoked to win superbowl games.

the belief of a need for an intermediary between divinity and humankind has delivered us into a profound state of disconnection, unworthiness, and war and is now reaching a deafening roar of subterfuge. quietly and consistently, it has slipped underneath the radar over thousands of years and stands now at the core of our current social structure. it is of paramount importance that we recognize this, for it is precisely this silent disconnection that guarantees the reign of fear and war all around the world.

in the past millennia, this amalgamation of religion-and-state was symbolized by the combustive spread of colonialism and imperialism. today, we have the contemporary face of tyranny: terrorism. and yet, whether state sponsored or by independent groups, it is only an exterior symptom. the true root of terror can be found only in one place: a deep and unabiding fear and powerlessness within the individual self **x** a government inflated by a super-power identity riddled with exploitive double standards = very dangerous times. freedom and security have become something we tenaciously cling to outside of us the more that we feel the fear rising inside of us. and the more panicked we become, the more desperately we seek to find an enemy who we can put a face to and destroy so that we can feel safe once again . . . but somehow it never happens. notice that the face of the bad guys keep changing. why? because there is no evil-bad-guy-enemy. there is but one enemy only: the ignorance of disconnection.

---

peace
cannot be kept by force,
it can only be achieved
by understanding.

>> albert einstein

---

here is breaking news: *no human being is entirely evil* . . . we are at war with our own darkness and disconnection. the human condition is now so disconnected from its own greatness and its own darkness that we either deify our leaders and celebrities on a huge pedestal as our celebrated golden girls and boys, or we demonize any public figure who transgresses even slightly as heinous and villainous . . . **when both are a lie.** we are living vicariously through each of them. do we not <u>all</u> have the capacity for greatness and darkness? all of humanity simply reflects our own self. *there is no such thing as an inferior or superior human being.* **there is no one who needs to be worshipped or destroyed.** to be connected to our own soul is to know this. to be disconnected from this truth is to be at war with ourselves and, therefore, each other. i beseech you to please think about this.

the words of the philosopher-kings of ancient times ring clearly in our world now more than ever: political unity without a spiritual dimension is meaningless. many have strived, but in vain, to ignite it. there have been a plentitude of great leaders throughout all of history seeking to awaken the same truth at the center of every religious faith: the singular core truth of love and unity, not hatred and destruction.

there is no such thing as the will of god declaring war. no war is holy. that is the will of man and how sadly we have been confused to blur this critical distinction.

>> one man with courage makes a majority. <<
andrew jackson

to claim holy righteousness and then kill and subjugate other human beings in the same breath is to plunge into the very abyss of darkness you intended to destroy, never comprehending that what you are doing to another, you are only doing to yourself. war has nothing to do with god, but it has indeed everything to do with political power built upon the absence of the soul.

our regime change starts right here, people.
look around: our anesthetized past is creating an extremely frightening future . . .

if we travel to the root in the united states, we find a nation built upon the idea of equality, but rife with layers of contradiction. in essence, our foundation of freedom was built upon the enslavement of our own people. clearly, the poisons and wounds of "arbitrary equality" have had a highly cancerous effect and has borne a deeply sad and bitter fruit. as a result of this condition, one of the most brilliant methods of invisible incarceration has been utilized and done so with astounding accuracy: ***the most efficient way to oppress a people is to silently teach them to oppress themselves.*** then, you are no longer culpable and at the same time will still reap all the rewards politically. i will demonstrate how efficiently this has been deployed: name the two groups most discriminated against throughout the last several hundred years = by a landslide it is people of color and women. so, why were these two groups of people such a threat to the governing power? simple. because they both possess immediate ties to the model of spirituality + state = unity, rather than religion + state = rule by domination, and thereby posed a major threat to the institutions of both religion and state who claimed they were the:
a) only and highest authority, and b) the sole way to access god.

the reason is this:
these two groups of people, women and people of color, were the first to ever-so-splendidly
embody self = soul = sole authority (as in having their own direct connection to divinity).

women have been revered throughout all of time because of their direct connection to the divine presence . . . in the holy power that dwells beneath their skin as their ability to bring forth life. and for people of color (in this country, the native americans and african americans), their roots run deep in indigenous ancestry. it is in this rich cultural tradition where it is acknowledged and celebrated that the divine presence lives in the earth and in our bodies instead of beyond it. of course, this was not only deeply feared when this country was born, but it was in direct opposition to our political structure of power (and, of course, to those who held it). therefore, it has historically followed that these groups of people must not only be silenced but actually taught to ingest a deep shame about the very quality that radiates so brightly their magnificence. and so began the mechanism of external and internal enslavement jointly. it is not too difficult to break the body, but it takes much more cunning to break the heart and spirit of a human being all at the same time.

and look how efficiently this method still works — these are the only two groups of people in history actually idealized for their powerlessness. in both groups, the very thing that in truth makes them so powerful has been completely reversed in our society: first, instead of the sexuality of women being venerated and honored as the vessel for life, women are sexually objectified / objectify themselves. women pimp themselves mostly: beauty / sexuality are used as a means to an end. it is spent as currency for women to get what they want. (visited beverly hills lately? those are the highest paid prostitutes you will ever meet.) for many of the most beautiful women, there is very little truth behind their beauty. it is literally used as a mask to manipulate. (need proof? just check back on these women's lives 30 years later. you will find an empty shell in full make-up.)

the sexuality of women sells everything from tools to music to athletes to "entertainment" in its many forms (pornography is a billion dollar industry); the river of self-loathing and self-disconnection runs very deep through anorexia, bulimia, breast implants, botox, collagen, liposuction, and a host of other parasites that pass under the masquerade of "beauty." the more unnatural, doll-ish and emaciated women are, the more beautiful they are, right? * bonus connect.the.dots: why is thin culturally lauded as *in?* because thin = androgyny = no curves / womanliness = disconnected from the creative force of the universe contained within a woman's body = **powerless.** it is the perfect socio-political catch 22. like that very-good-movie says, real women *do* have curves (at whatever weight a woman is). yet, think about it, women are literally starving — in every sense — to be desirable and wanted by others. for women, sexual desirability = power, right??? ok, right about now would be a good time for our field trip to that strip club. women need to wake up. exploiting our own sexuality for gain does not mean "we have beaten men at their own game." it means we have betrayed ourselves, become our own captor, and given away the key. *it is not unnatural for women to be beautiful and truly powerful . . .*
it is unnatural that women have forgotten how.

then, for people of color, this inversion of power is equally deft. instead of being honored for their inherent indigenous and ancient connection to the wisdom of the spiritual, they are instead expected by many people in this country (who think it but dare not speak it) to become the opposite: some warped modern versions of minstrels as athletes or entertainers . . . i.e., to journey from wise man to fool. or, as in the case of the native americans — to go from being everywhere across this beautiful nation to now becoming nearly extinct and invisible.

the castration of the authentic nature of a people results in the slow dimming of the collective memory of their true ancestral heritage, eventually resulting in a state of economic and political powerlessness (e.g., our ghettoes and reservations). an example: "so, you want to be successful, young man?" well, just make sure you are playing "black music" (meaning rap / "soul! music"), or "black sports" (meaning basketball / football) with all of those entities owned primarily by people who are not african american, fyi. and for those who manage to step outside that familiar box of cultural predetermination, such as tiger woods, the death threats get lost in the applause. it is also very common to hear today from someone of several shades lighter skin (as they slather on self-tanner by the gallon), "what is so bad about people thinking you have rhythm or can jump high? i mean, i'm not prejudiced — i have friends who are black, but, well, you know, they don't act black." my, my, how interesting. i wonder — have you visited www.blackpeopleloveus.com?? (i suggest you check it out pronto if u have not.) and what is, i beg the question, the exact way that black people (or any people) are supposed to act like? if you are born with certain features — does that automatically mean you will possess a certain vocabulary or work at a casino on a reservation? or if you are born a woman, use your body as a sexual weapon??

prejudice (to literally pre-judge the value of another human being) is so accepted in our culture that we do not even notice it anymore. discrimination has morphed during the last hundred years from a language of words spoken outright of hate and human devaluation to the thoughts of silent and deadly agreement of the same inhumane supposition. the language has become audibly imperceptible; yet, it is spoken in every single place you look. it is seen but not heard. racism has not improved. **it has simply gone underground.**

>> he who controls the past controls the future. he who controls the present controls the past. <<
george orwell, *1984*

this *pseudo-assimilation* is why it has become so easy for the expressions of these cultures to be commercialized by others for their own profit to sell music, clothing, or anything else for that matter. it is exploitation disguised as originality. it is a cultural rape of the expression of a people masquerading as a love affair. there is no ownership, because there has never been any legitimate honoring and healing of our collective past. perhaps, this is why the film *bamboozled* made people a little too uncomfortable, (bless u, spike lee, for speaking the truth).

and yet, both groups are continually told: "it's an equal playing field now, so get over it already" . . . and to that i say to the person speaking, "please, really, you first." if it only were that simple, it would have been done already. there remains still a past that haunts us today lurking right beneath the surface . . . a past of human devaluation and murderous brutality from hundreds of years connected to these two groups of people that have never been resolved or addressed. therefore, it never really went away — it just went underground and into the collective psyche where it has embedded itself undisturbed . . . until now.

awareness brings a radical awakening of consciousness, especially in this case.
this is a place our society clearly needs very deep healing.

>> one of our strongest weapons is dialogue. <<
nelson mandela

as we continue to go2theroot: the state of our "national family," of varying sibling groups of ethnicities and communities, in many ways, reflects our nuclear family structure (or lack of) in this nation. there is the same finger pointing and "you don't understand what it was like for me" — as if someone can win the "but-my-pain-was-the-greatest" contest, followed by the familiar resentment and retreat to our bedrooms (or our communities), as the case may be. observe how the same thing occurs in most families: nothing ever gets resolved because nothing has ever been addressed or healed from the past. we just act like it isn't there anymore. either that, or we rage against the machine wanting to destroy the enemy. this is equally futile. **the natural law is this: what you hate and fight against, you shall eventually become.** the only true liberation is one that heals the oppressed and the oppressor at the same time (gandhi spoke this concept many times). it is critical to understand that this is definitely not just an issue of black and white, or men and women. this is about every kind of people, every kind of history, from every kind of nation on the planet. there is deep wisdom beneath the wounding in every culture that exists and that is waiting to be awakened and translated for the future of our world. the united states simply provides a potent template for this possibility. it is a nation that contains a shining promise of democracy and equality that dares to be fulfilled. the legacy of its past and future echoes loudly as the entire world is reminded: the power of true leadership is to lead by example.

connect.the.dots. we will never come to peace with any other country until we heal in our own nation(s). as long as hatred is an acceptable way to treat each other with our socially stratified ghettos, desolate native american reservations, and "our mexican immigrant situation" — all living in third world conditions down the street from million dollar mansions (oh, just one example) — then, hatred and war will continue to be what we give to the world. and, of course, we will receive even greater amounts of it returned to us — it is natural law that what you give you shall receive. such is the political law of gravity: what goes up, must come down. and to be absolutely and perfectly clear, we cannot continue at the rate we are going.

>> hate never yet dispelled hate. only love dispels hate. this is the law — ancient and inexhaustible. <<
gautama buddha

we are fighting with those who are most like us . . . we destroy in each other what we cannot face in ourselves: (hello, arabs and jews!?) have we learned nothing from the middle east? blind denial combined with violence have taken us to the end of the road people. war + war = more war. an eye for an eye leaves all of us blind. we must deal with what is at the root in each one of our countries *and what is at the root in each one of our lives.* and let it be said: the truth is a volcano that is about to erupt everywhere in the world. this is our call to action. **we cannot bring peace to any other country if we cannot bring peace to ourselves.** that is the only true precursor to a reality of soul + state = unity around the world. there must be a willingness to heal from all parties involved. this is the only way to create a future worth living in, for our families, for our nations, and for ourselves. and this transformation happens with the willingness of just one person at a time . . . which, of course, brings us back to you. all of this is extremely relevant to your own life and the "adventure to power" you just underwent. in fact, there is a p r o f o u n d connection between what you just read and your own life . . . can you guess what it might be?

true compassion is equally needed as healing for our world and for the individual.

---

the elixir is hidden in the poison.   >> rumi

>> humankind must evolve for all human conflict a method that rejects revenge, aggression, and retaliation. the foundation of such a method is love. <<

dr. martin luther king, jr.

> **go2theroot:**
> if all the world were connected to their own soul = their own humanity,
> we could honor, with compassion, the humanity of the rest of the world —
> regardless of religious and cultural distinctions.
> being connected to the soul transcends religious barrier. think about it.
> most of the world knows the concept of the divine as *outside of themselves* . . .
> and that is the only reason why they can justify killing other human beings.
>
> **perhaps, if we could accept the oneness of god, then perhaps, too,**
> **we could accept in reality the oneness of humankind —**
> **and cease to measure, and hinder, and harm others in terms of their differences . . .**
> **>> malcolm x, after he returned from his pilgrimage to mecca**

(true) compassion is literally translated as "together with — feel deeply" =
the wisdom and fire of the heart = the simultaneous recognition of the truth
and the burning away of what is not the truth.
<> *all* life as sacred and equal and all emotion is honored as valuable
<> connected to the soul = divinity / authority **within** us
　　(+ let it be known: "compassion" in hebrew means "womb")

(false) / old definition of compassion = "to lower ourselves — suffer with"
sympathy = pity on those beneath us = the agreement of victimhood
by one's pain / emotions = to devalue emotion and denigrate it
<> see human life as either inferior or superior
<> disconnected from the soul = divinity / authority **outside** of us

> **compassion in action** is the capacity to truly hear and to honor the truth
> of the individual / collective heart. humanity has only one heart with many faces.

> **>> humanity is one. religion is one. truth is one. <<**

dadaji

fight the power, **or find** the power**?**
(marvin is still waiting on us to answer what's really goin on . . . !?)
connect.the.dots
subject → activists

to begin, think of some of the more extreme activist groups in recent history
(examples: militant anti-abortion protesters, feminists who are anti-men, reparationists, etc.).
next, in your journal, make a list of the things that you are the most opposed to / against
in the world. what are things that are totally socially intolerable to you and reeeally get you upset?
what are your hot buttons?

ok now, examine what is the distinction between
fighting **against** — **anti** something <u>vs.</u> standing **for** something?
which is more effective in the grand scheme of things?
here is the million dollar q: how is either stance reflective of what is happening at the root
in that person's (activist's) heart? for example: the violent peace protester(!)

as we just read a quote from malcolm x — a very militant activist — who, after traveling
on a spiritual pilgrimage, underwent a profound transformation in his heart
from anger to wisdom and, therefore, radically altered his entire ideology.

now take out the list you made about your own hot button issues.
go2theroot:
see what it reflects that you feel you must fight against in your own life and why.

>> when i discover who i am, i'll be free. <<
ralph ellison

for example: i used to absolutely detest anywhere where women were objectified.
to say it was my hot button would be an understatement. (background → at age 18 was also a boxer =
would pick fights with men who would make lewd comments to me while, say, crossing the street.)
it was not until i recovered the truth and power of my womanhood that i understood why i was
enraged at and reacted so violently to the world. i was fighting the untruth in my own heart
about the value of a woman. when i connected to the truth in myself, i freed myself and rejoiced.
and now i am a **womanist** (more on that later).

my question to you is: what is it that you stand for? look at the power of what it is to stand
for the truth *that is at the root of what you are fighting against* in yourself. indeed, we are always
sent exactly what we need to awaken us to our own gifts . . . our greatest healing = our greatest gifts.
(*if* we have the courage to complete our circle of soul initiation, that is.) of course, choosing to stay
pissed off is always an option, too. just accept your effectiveness at living your soul, and
affecting the world is greatly reduced. this is what it means, in very practical terms,
to be the change you want to see in the world.
this is what it is to be **a love souldier**.

> soulfire is about love as a political force.

>> am i not destroying my enemies when i make friends of them? <<
abraham lincoln

assignment:

honoring the truth of my own heart = **the liberation declaration**

a:
reading back over your adventure to power, pick one individual who had the most wounding impact on your heart and on your life. when was your heart broken open? what is the one relationship in your life where you have felt the most pain? tell yourself the truth: **who is it?** what was the core emotion you experienced as a result? take that emotion to the emotional spectrum below:

neutral

+ 8	+ 6	+ 4	+ 2	− 2	− 4	− 6	− 8
self-worth / unconditional love	compassion	honor self	acceptance	judgment	betrayal	anger	unworthy of being loved / hatred

find where your emotion would be on the spectrum. then, match it to the one corresponding on the other end of the spectrum → set this aside for a moment.

fact:
no one comes into our lives with only one side of the spectrum:
they come to awaken us into wholeness with ourselves . . .

our emotions are sacred messengers from our soul to our heart

>> the course of human history is determined, not by what happens in the skies, but what takes place in our hearts. <<
sir arthur keith

the gifts of our soul are often awakened through the doorway of our emotions
our soul speaks to us through our heart . . .
if our hearts are numb, we will not hear our soul speaking

in order to receive this blessing, we must understand
how forgiveness and compassion work together:

> forgiveness is always for the "who," not the "what."

you are connecting from your heart to the heart of another = the purity and presence of truth
and love connect. and compassion can then happen because you can see yourself in the eyes
of whom you are forgiving. this is unity in action.

> you must always forgive yourself first before you forgive another.
this is the key to liberation in all things personal and political.

the three levels of forgiveness:

1) self
2) immediate circle who wounded you
3) collective wounding

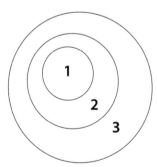

+ anything unforgiven is held in the body (we will explore this later on).

>> [there is] no future without forgiveness. <<
archbishop desmond tutu (book title)

example:
if you try to forgive someone for hurting you, you must first forgive yourself
for accepting / believing that what they said was the truth about you . . .
then and only then can you forgive them and release them from your heart.

we are afraid that if we feel what is most painful in us . . .
then it must really be the truth about us. *it must.*
(that we really are unworthy or unlovable.)

fact:
the more painful an emotion is —
the more that the truth / your true self has been suppressed behind it.
the truth only hurts when we are disconnected from it.
when we connect to it, the truth heals us. and, hence,
the truth shall set you free . . .

that is why compassion and forgiveness are so strong together!
as you feel what you are most afraid of / what others told you about you →
the fire of your heart literally explodes open the walls around it — because at the same time —
compassion acknowledges the truth underneath the wound as you are forgiving yourself
for believing what is false and for having silenced who you truly are. as you do this,
you are also acknowledging and grounding yourself in self-truth in that same moment.

there is nothing more painful in life than in being a victim
to the disconnection from our own heart and soul.

it is to also know . . .
that the only person who can ever liberate you is yourself.

**the true voice of your heart is always compassionate and neutral.
the voice of truth just is — it never has to prove anything.**

b:
light a candle and sit in silence — for as long as you need to — to do this: in your journal, write a letter to yourself asking forgiveness for where you have given pieces of your *self* away and believed anything that is not the truth about you. (this is a practice you will use for the rest of your life.)

example of how this might look:
{dear me},
i am so sorry for believing that i do not deserve love because mom always said no one would ever love me, and i believed her. please forgive me for being so hateful to myself all these years. i am so sorry . . .
it is not the truth about me.

>> you are never powerless. <<
jane seymour

c:

go back to the emotion that you matched on the spectrum above now.

what is the emotion that it matched up with? this is the gift of truth that this person brought into your life as it was called out from your soul to be awakened in you . . .

in your journal or on a separate piece of paper, write a letter *to the heart* of the person you were most wounded by.

give yourself full permission to say whatever you may need to; end it with "i forgive you and release you. with grace and with gratitude, i receive the blessing and love you have opened me to." you may choose to burn these letters and say a prayer afterwards, or rip them up, or put them away. do what feels right. whatever that is, you will know.

our family and those closest to us are here to teach us how to love . . .
ourselves and each other.
when we understand this, we are truly free.

>> if we could read the secret history of our enemies, we should find in each person's life, sorrow and suffering, enough to disarm all hostility. <<
henry wadsworth longfellow

give yourself the time you need to complete this. the more you are able to do this with unexpressed
pain that you have from anyone in your past . . . the more energy you will free up for your future.
at any moment, we can always choose to liberate the past or the future.

wisdom
is seeing the love people are trying to give
that is trapped behind and beneath all of their wounds.
mastery
is being able to receive it.

just for a moment . . . *imagine the impact it would have if families read this book,
or if nations could utilize these principles on their deepest wounds???*

there is no power greater than love. it transforms all things.

you just traveled from powerlessness to power — how does it feel, pioneer?
good work!! what an immense gift you have just received from yourself.
now, please, go relax and enjoy this amazing day!!!
you may want to take a long bath, or a nap,
or perhaps go to the day spa or to an afro-brazilian dance class . . .
(some of my favorite things after i have had a heart exploding experience of
self-connection). this is the wonder of life —
there is truly no limit to the amount of love you can give and receive.

the heart allways knows the truth.

>> just knowing has meant everything to me. <<
alice walker

self compassion

stage five: movement — opening to grace

you **cannot**
avoid **paradise,**
you **can only**
avoid **seeing it.**

>> charlotte joko beck

suggested soulfire soundtracks for this section:
<> audra mcdonald: *way back to paradise*   <> samuel barber: *adagio for strings*
<> flora purim: *perpetual emotion*   <> n'dea davenport: (self-titled)
<> kenny loggins: *leap of faith*   <> stevie wonder: *journey through the secret life of plants*
<> hot water music: *no division*   <> annie lennox: *bare*

suggested soulfire fieldtrip destinations for this section:
<> pick some wildflowers, then plant some more   <> go to a poetry reading
<> go skinny dipping in a waterfall   <> walk in the rain — naked if you dare
(yes, i have done all of these things — in case u were wondering)

aliveness:
the freedom to experience and celebrate the full spectrum of what it is to be alive.

by this definition, if we looked around our world, it would seem that there are many who are the walking dead: frozen, numb, and afraid to feel. (not to mention oblivious to their soul.) "how are you doing today?" is rotely answered with an emphatic "great!" — while that same person just came from the doctor who has warned them for the eighth time about their high blood pressure, and their cell phone is ringing with their daughter calling from the rehab clinic (again), and add to that they haven't really slept for the last six days — "but really, things are great. i am really very happy. really, i am. i mean, really" (never realizing it is ourselves we are desperately trying to convince). shutting down our emotions can render a person lifeless faster than you can clap your hands. yet, this is the way most of us live because, at least, it is better than the alternative . . . well, you know . . . emotional insanity. (and we've all seen a variety of examples of this.) what we have not seen very often, however, is the possibility that you can feel your emotions deeply — yes, all of them — and still be very grounded, calm, and actually alivened by them.

this would preclude one gigantic elephant in the room: denial. we are a culture of denial and disconnection. we can be a country at war and still be more interested in the golden globe awards. it takes our children shooting up their schools, classmates and teachers, and then finding out our husband is gay before we notice something might actually be awry at home. we will celebrate diversity, while hate crimes are happening down the street. we have accepted, as a cultural norm, to pop anti-depressants as if they are happy vitamins. we are constantly raving about our robust economy, but please don't mention our homeless and hungry population or the suicide rate of children on native american reservations.

>> if one is out of touch with oneself, then one cannot touch others. <<
anne morrow lindbergh

we marvel at our latest medical advances and then leave the room when the subject turns to our system of healthcare . . . and what of those who try to get our attention, like the music of (some) heavy metal / rap? it is terrible — so just ban it! really! who could write such violent lyrics?!! (perhaps we should begin to consider that what could cause someone to write about such extreme violence is the fact that they are probably drowning in it . . . go2theroot.) we have been adept at silencing the messenger, because as you are now catching on, we have been very adept at silencing ourselves.
case in point: for many people, anxiety attacks are but one thing: **soul earthquakes.** ironically, it is only when we numb our emotions that they do the very thing we are most afraid of — they implode upon us with overwhelming velocity . . . just turn on the evening news and watch it with new eyes. witness collective implosion. contrary to popular belief and effort, it is not possible to stick ourselves on the happy button and remain there indefinitely. there is nothing about living behind an unmoving and unfeeling mask that relates to true happiness. that is what is actually known as "a living hell."
a pretty prison is still a prison any way you look at it.

life, in all of its wisdom, brings us many colors on the emotional spectrum and asks us to receive them all with an open heart and open eyes. this is genuinely what it is to open to grace, and it brings us something much richer than the frozen happiness button. it brings us a wild illumined openness to ourselves and to feeling all of the mystery of what it is to be alive . . . and that is truly a miracle.

to review, emotions, *every single kind*, are sacred messengers from our soul to our hearts to awaken us to the true purpose of our life. let's go deeper with this. what other gifts of your soul have you been awakened to through experiences that have brought very powerful emotions in their wake?

>> those who don't know how to weep with their whole heart, don't know how to laugh either. <<
golda meir

right now, witness your life as if you are watching a movie and look at your entire family, your childhood, where and how you grew up, all of it . . . and view it all from the perspective of your own soul. is it possible that your whole life has been conspiring to prepare and awaken you to who you truly are? is it inconceivable to think your soul knew the kind of life it was going to be born into and that it chose your particular family and life to do it? how this particular environment would give you everything you need, all the perfect ingredients and catalysts for the awakening to the purpose of your own life? the brilliance and intelligence of the universe is present in everything it creates — did you really think you would be the only one out of the whole planet forgotten and overlooked? and even beyond this, what if the divine presence of this universe has so much faith in your becoming that it is constantly trying to communicate with you the only way it can — through sending you experiences that impact and open you to your own heart? just living the good life means nothing to the soul. it is not impressed. why are you here now? it wants you to know and it wants you to listen. and it will communicate with you any way you let it. just look back at your life and you will see the writing on the wall from your own soul to you. breathe and hear this: what has it been trying to tell you?

even the most bitter cynic will be able to feel the truth in these words . . .
for even the coldest hearts can always be melted to feel the presence of love once again.
(i am tempted to use mr. winter warlock in *santa claus is coming to town* here
but be glad i am leaving you to think of your own examples of this.)

your soul already knows where it is going . . .
it possesses the map to your destiny.
you are simply along for the ride.
so, the question remains: are you going to fight joy or celebrate it?
how you live your life is, in essence, a tribute to either one choice or the other.

>> to find the good life you must become yourself. <<
dr. bill jackson

78

your soul wants nothing more than your greatest joy and deepest aliveness.
and, by the way, you will never be smarter than it is, so stop killing yourself
trying to figure it all out. you will only exhaust yourself and annoy others.
this is why all enlightened beings are always laughing.

there are messages of truth about who you are in every single emotion . . .
fear included!!!
(note: do not kill the messenger! thank it and listen to it!)
< you must first honor your emotions as sacred before you can decode them >

your greatest healing is the doorway to your greatest gifts.

there is no shame in tears. when they are honest, they are one
of the most precious and beautiful things in the world.

life is not punishment; it is an awakening.

underneath all things is the truth.
the truth is always love.

———————————————————

embracing
the purpose of all things as love
is to know the essence of
faith

———————————————————

faith brings unconditional peace and wisdom.
allways remember e.h.f.a.r. = **e**verything **h**appens **for a r**eason.

**it is to understand that all of life is meant only to return you
to the truth within you.**

>> there are things that are known, and things that are unknown. in between there are doors. <<

william blake

assignment:

you want the truth? you *can* handle the truth: the truth is love.

a:
begin to decode all of your self-talk from the language of self-judgment, and translate it into the language of self-compassion — especially where your emotions are concerned. practice telling (*first yourself*, then others) the absolute and real truth about how you feel. all the time. at first, this may seem grueling, but hang in there — it will become natural and something you will actually cherish and trust deeply, in time. our connection to the truth is the most valuable thing in life. know this.

true intimacy occurs with the ability to be vulnerable with yourself in the presence of another person. this is not spilling your guts in an act of patheticism. it is the real vulnerability and deep strength that comes with groundedness. suddenly, you will find speaking your truth is like giving a gift. it does not matter if someone chooses to unwrap your present or not. what matters is that you gave something truly beautyfull . . . and that can never be diminished.
speaking the truth honors all.

try this: go on strike for the truth in your life.
this is a revolutionary act, for our world is drowning in untruth.

b:

your soul family tree (yes, soul is thicker than blood)

draw a family tree where everyone who is on it are people that have come into your life, each bearing a specific and significant fruit, that have awakened you to your own heart and soul. your soul has an actual frequency, just like a radio station signal, that has drawn many into your life for this singular purpose . . . creating your soul family tree is a very cool way to see the brilliance of the unfoldment of your life + to acknowledge all the beautiful fruits / gifts you have received. and it usually inspires a sense of awe and often quite a few tears. yes, you can admit it . . . your soul is the love bazeeyomb. (but i am already knowing this: you are the reason this book has been written. *can u feel* how big i am smiling right now???)

---

ponder how your soul has drawn every single thing that has ever happened in your life to you. this is the fast track way to experiencing extreme grace and gratitude in life.

>> fear grows out of the things we think; it lives in our minds. compassion grows out of the things we are, and lives in our hearts. <<

barbara garrison

self compassion

stage six: the becoming — integration

many of us spend our whole lives running from feeling with the mistaken belief that you can not bear the pain. but you have already borne the pain. what you have not done is feel all you are beyond that pain.

>> kahlil gibran

suggested soulfire soundtracks for this section:
<> emma shaplin: *carmine deo*   <> sting: *mercury falling*
<> incognito: *100 degrees and rising*   <> the brand new heavies: *brother sister*
<> bjork: *homogenic*   <> seal: *human being*   <> ephraim lewis: *skin*

suggested soulfire fieldtrip destinations for this section:
<> hike in some enchanted mountains   <> take a trip to the zoo
<> watch the movie *behind the sun*   <> go dancing   <> + when in doubt, karaoke

stop reading right now and answer this question: how do you feel right now?

how did you arrive at your answer? for most people the answer is generated as an assessment from their mind. but guess what, i have a little news flash for you — that is not what you feel; it is what you think you feel. and there is no such thing. you cannot think your feelings. you can only feel them. dern. (bringing the head and heart in balance we will explore next.) most of us skip the most vital step to experiencing our feelings and that is: stage moja (= swahili for stage one) going within the body. this is the first place we become aware of our emotions. to review, when we learned about the grounded state, we understood that the body is the access point from our outer to inner world. recall also, when we worked with forgiveness, we also discovered that whatever is unforgiven is still held in our body. this is also the case for whatever is unexpressed in our life; it is also contained in the body as energy waiting and wanting to be expressed. if we have learned nothing else from this entire process — we know this: whatever is not expressed in our life does not go away. it just changes form and asks (or demands, as the case may be,) our attention to it somewhere else in our life.

ok. you are probably wondering what to do with that piece of information? ("i have things unexpressed from 1987! now what?") not to worry. first, so does most of the world. and, second, just keep reading because you are in good hands.

there are two monumentally effective ways to release energy that is stuck. and for the record, when i say "energy," i mean the life force present in an individual. for instance, you may have a tremendous amount of grief or anger that you have never expressed in your life and instead have, say, constant headaches or stomach pain. this is your body's way of saying, "please listen — i have something you need to acknowledge and express. this is not supposed to be stuck in here, so get this out of me now!!!!"

>> you need to claim the events of your life to make yourself yours. <<
florida scott maxwell

and here is the magic secret:
movement and sound release blocked energy

be inventive here. there a million ways to apply this. i am going to give you a powerful one in your assignment; however, this is no substitute for your own exploration. (ok, ok, some more examples: after an argument with the one you love where your tongue was tied and you said all the wrong things . . . in the car, on the way home alone, yell everything you really wanted to say. the essence of what that is will often suddenly become very clear to you. another — if you come home from work very angry and are home alone, put on some heavy metal or some excellent punk rock and dance it out aggressively for 5 minutes. you will feel much, much better and will actually have much more energy now that you freed up all that was suppressed.)

the more you learn to honor yourself, the more you will give yourself what you need when you need it, and the more your self-expression will, in turn, honor you. bonus — no more crying at office meetings and no more going off on the poor kids. (pleeez, *no more drama!!* in fact, declare your life a drama-free zone asap.) hint: where there is drama, there is always conflict between the life and the soul of the one who has started it. newsflash: your life is not the place to fling everything unresolved within you. **stop blaming and start claiming!**

the body is truly our greatest teacher in life. the more connected you become to it, the easier it is to access exactly how you are feeling in any given moment.

>> and the day came when the risk to remain tight in a bud was more painful than the risk it took to blossom. <<
anaïs nin

all emotions are equally worthy of acceptance <> wholeness brings peace

what is that you say: "peace?? peace?? where do i find that?" everyone in the world is telling us
the secret to success is to "take control of your life,"
and "get it together," right??
wrong.

hint: the big secret to life is that control is a myth. sorry, janet.
control is what we settle for when we are soulfire-less and lost, except that we keep driving,
convinced we know where we are going. the more disconnected and anxious we become,
the more often we refuse to stop at the gas station of our soul to ask for directions . . .
(a comic but tragically accurate metaphor for most of the world, and, yes,
even for most successful people. in fact, success too often spells disaster
if the soul is m.i.a.) control = holding on, maintaining image.
true freedom = letting go, maintaining soul.
take your pick.

freedom comes only from an inner knowing and calm built upon firm self-connection.
it is the opposite of needing to control. it is the acceptance of what is and the ability to relax.
it honors and trusts deeply the divine purpose and true perfection in all things. **this is true peace.**
and this is the place to take action from in one's life. (everything else is just a band-aid.
and though that is currently the trend, it is not the solution.)

consider yourself a surgeon for the truth. learn to extract it.

begin to cultivate your "witness self": it is your own unbiased sports commentator
who sees every single thing happening in front of you without reacting to it.
it allows you to see the truth and then, calmly and clearly, create from it.
(fyi — this is where you must remember to stop, drop, and breathe.)

your consciousness = the eyes of your soul, which are the heart of awareness within you.
it is your inborn capacity to be fully present to life. every moment of it.
it is to know the sun in the sky and the truth in your life with the same conviction.

explore what it would literally feel like to surrender to your soul

---

the opening heart is the most beautiful flower of all.
the greatest beauty in the world is compassion, love shining free
of attachment and grasping.   >> tarthang tulka

>> the rhythm of my heart is the birth and death of all that is alive. <<
thich nhat hanh

assignment:

ritual of release / permission to express

what have you not given yourself permission to feel in your life? to express? what have you not accepted in yourself, and what is the core emotion underneath it?

> make a list of the five things that resonate most deeply for what emotions you have not been able to express in your life (examples: anger, sadness, betrayal, etc.).

> take this list and go out in nature → to the beach or hike up somewhere overlooking a hillside or vista. either location, ensure that no one is in the immediate vicinity. pick up five rocks or shells, ideally the size of a baseball. let each object symbolize something you have never expressed in your life.

> take your time to center your breath, and then state your intention for release.

> one by one, pick up each object and hold it to the place in your body you most feel the energy pulsating. slowly feel a sound begin to build of how that emotion feels in your body and in your life . . .

> when you are ready, yell that sound until there is no more sound left and then throw the object as far away as possible. continue with each one until you are done. your intention is everything here . . . how much you want to be free of these things (that you have been invisibly dragging behind you) will determine how much energy actually leaves your body.

>> i am here to live aloud. <<

emile zola

as you do this assignment, you are reclaiming the pieces of yourself that have been held hostage by your past. this is true bondage . . . and you have just granted yourself the sweet freedom of acceptance.

to know love is to know freedom.

wisdom compass:

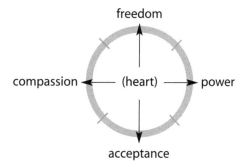

>> stop thinking and talking about it, and there is nothing you will not be able to know. <<
zen paradigm

for journaling:
what does freedom mean to you?
imagine that your most wildly alive and connected self is a country (name it), or use your name
(____-land). what would your self-government be like? make a flag of freedom for your country with
symbols on it that represent your **soulfire.**

> what language would be spoken? what holidays would you have?

> what currency / economic system would you use? socialist-capitalism perhaps? i propose this as an
integrated economic model that is a synthesis of the truth contained within the two extremes that
these models symbolize: a free trade market combined with an environment where everyone works
in careers that serve the highest good of their own soul = the highest good of humanity.
this is a win-win in the purest sense.

> what would your entertainment industry be like? what if the music industry produced music instead
of strippers? or if hollywood understood the tremendous opportunity it has to illuminate instead of
glorifying darkness? just a thought.

> education system? maybe this might mean schools in the ghetto might actually get funding instead
of more liquor stores selling eight-ball — gasp! that *would* be a shock. going to the root here means
that we realize it is not about "no more eight ball," but that it is about the fundamental devaluation of
life for certain groups of people who, many, in positions of power, still to this day, silently, yet actively
support. *unity must precede diversity.* the root of this is not only about why people of color have come
to accept this as just 'the way it is', it is also about why people of euro-centric descent are so afraid of
themselves that they must discriminate against anyone who reflects what they cannot access.

fact: **hatred begins in the self.** the root of racism is disconnection from our own humanity. to disconnect and devalue the humanity of another is only *the symptom* of racism. so how can education impact this? how about those school textbooks that serve the interests of the equivalent to a special interest lobbying group that teaches our youth what they want them to know vs. the actual truth?

> justice system? give some serious thought to this one. remember there actually is a distinction between the "who" (the divinity within all human beings) and the "what" (the choices one makes based upon their own consciousness). we cannot look at one without the other. note: a sign of tyranny is when the whole of existence is reduced to being either all good or all evil, when in truth, all of humanity has the capacity for both. two words here: **free will.** every soul has divinity and every person has free will to remember or forget it . . . violently evil acts occur when people are grossly disconnected.
soo, how would you construct a justice system that brings both truth and transformation?

go2theroot . . .
how are the political and the spiritual, at their essence, the same thing? how does this apply to our past, present, and future political condition? as people begin to structure their lives by the purpose of their soul = living for the highest good of their life . . . discuss how government can reflect this by being structured for the highest good of all. (what an extraordinary concept!?) discuss how this is contingent upon each person being connected to their own highest good for governments to shift domestically and globally. note: the current state of our government(s) and leadership are not the problem. they are merely the sum of the disconnection in the masses. consider: what would it be like to have a governing structure that inspires the masses instead of ruling them? lastly, define the meaning of freedom for the individual and for the collective. connect.the.dots between them. how does one impact the other?

>> because of our routines, we forget that life is an ongoing adventure. <<
maya angelou

socrates said: may the inner and outer man be as one.
such is true be-u-ty and health.

imagine what would happen if, as a society, we stopped spending billions and billions of dollars
a year on diets and workout gear and instead looked at what is unexpressed and what
is being stored in our bodies. this is often at the root of excess weight and disease. the body
is an energy system that distributes weight according to your state. truly, your state creates
your life. excess weight is, often, excess wait and energetic insulation. what are you waiting
to let go of in your body that symbolizes what you want to release in your life? what parts
of your body feel like you are wearing armor? for women, it is no accident that we store most
of our weight around our womb (midsection) and sexual center (hips + thighs), *and* that
we have an epidemic of breast cancer and uterine-ovarian-cervical cancer. in addition, for men,
it is no accident that a top health danger is heart disease. connect.the.dots. we must cease
chasing the treadmill of symptoms and travel instead to the root of what is going on in
our bodies and what they are communicating to us. please hear this:
our bodies speak the voice of our soul.
to understand this is the only way to truly and permanently honor and change
your body and your health. the cool waters of self-compassion are drastically
needed here. expressing yourself and your feelings + diet and exercise become a
natural way of living when you know that the body is a temple of purity
and innocence that houses your soul. would you pollute a church?
yet, this is exactly what we do, and, sometimes, we do much worse.
we have forgotten that the body is the expression of the soul.
(secret: when you know this, exercise can be celebration instead of drudgery)

connect.the.dots . . . + new meaning to the words "it's all good."

ok, recap: we know that all emotions are sacred messengers from the soul
that speak to us through our body and our heart . . . that there is no such thing
as a "bad" emotion. even fear is a message to deepen our self-connection.
it truly is all good, because it is *all* guidance. that said, what would
it look like to honor your emotions all the time as sacred messengers . . .
(do you yell at the fedex man???) first, receive the message and then honor
it by taking the action you are guided towards and then, **wow** . . .
prepare for the feeling of the wild aliveness that comes from living your soul.
heehee. (that is the sound of glee.)

our life is but one adventure into soul-connection
(and you can always go deeper).

discuss how, when connected, emotions are the doorway to power.
and how, when disconnected, they are the doorway to darkness.
how does this show up all over our world?

(p.s. are you ready for self-fire to burst you into flames???? ok, just checking . . .)

>> my obligation is this: to be transparent. <<
pablo neruda

self-fire + fearlessness = watch out now

when i dare to be powerful, to use my strength in the service of my vision,
it becomes less and less important whether i am afraid.   >> audre lord

let's talk about fearlessness: is it possible to be fearless? big smile = oh yes.
(remember back to the intro? . . . the big scary dragons a.k.a. your fear.) well, our poor dragon
is looking more like a puppy dog because, as we bring truth, the shadow dissolves . . .
meaning → fear only comes hand-in-hand with disconnection. therefore, the more connected
we are, the more fear fades. so . . . what is an immediate way to connect in any given moment?
willingness.

this is your secret weapon. ground, breathe, affirm your willingness to trust + live
your soul, and then watch the magic and wisdom of the ancients fill you.
your self-fire will only serve to further illuminate you.

observe:

by standing on his own
a man finds happiness.

by standing on his own
a man finds freedom.

by standing on his own
he goes beyond the world.

by standing on his own
he finds the end of the way.

mastery always comes naturally
to the man who is wise and who loves himself.

the man who knows the truth
is never unhappy in the world.

i sit in my own radiance, and i have no fear.

>> the ashtavakra gita, an ancient sanskrit sacred text

the phrase "do not be afraid" recurs 365 times in the bible.

selffire

stage seven: nourishment — feeding the flames of your soulfire

you are what your deep, driving desire is. as is your desire,
so is your will. as is your will, so is your deed.
as is your deed, so is your destiny.

>> the upanishads

suggested soulfire soundtracks for this section:

<> peter gabriel: *passion*   <> buckshot lefonque: *music evolution*

<> fatala: *gongoma times*   <> jon hassell: *fascinoma*   <> debussy: *piano works vol. I*

<> ella fitzgerald: *something to live for*   <> prince: (alllll of it)

suggested soulfire fieldtrip destinations for this section:

<> rent *fight club* and watch it again   <> volunteer at a homeless shelter

<> visit an art gallery   <> people-watch at the mall during a big sale

passion ... desire ... hunger ... yearning ... doesn't sound very spiritual. in fact, it sounds downright like it is probably the source of our demise. hello, remember the movie *thornbirds!?* those are all the things that always get us into trouble. really, what could desire possibly have to do with the soul? oh, i don't know — mmmaybe just about everything. now, i am talking about pure desire here: defined as that which serves love (what serves the highest good of one serves the highest good of all). in contrast, we are accustomed to see "desire" mean something else, say, things that serve our disconnected self and selfishness. that is the other kind of desire. and the kind most of us know well."

even false desire is not our enemy but desire that is true and comes from the soul that gets repressed ... now, *that* is a "danger ... will robinson! danger" enemy. the fire of love within you can feel as explosive as a caged tiger if it is silenced. and as we just discovered, there is a whooooole lot that we are very accustomed to silencing and not expressing. now imagine this — for everything that was unexpressed on the dark side of the emotional spectrum, there are equal amounts on the light side of the passion of your soul that are waiting and wanting to be released.(!) hold onto your hats, because the force unleashed here is what is responsible for some of the most powerful and brilliant creations in history.

the passion of the soul is something rarely spoken of in our culture; yet, its presence is the surefire key to ultimate and exquisite joy and fulfillment in life. and its absence of it is, well, at the source of quite a few disturbing things in our world. observe: two of our most dire cultural epidemics are depression and debt. and both are directly linked to the repression of the soul's desires.

>> too many wish to be happy before becoming wise. <<
susanne curchod necker

the amount of debt is often connected to the amount of one's true life that is unlived = endless buying. (need i remind you of *fight club?* quick refresher from our ol' pal tyler dearden:"you are not your job. you are not how much you have in the bank. you are not the contents of your wallet.") f.c. is a timely wake up call, n'est pas? consumerism + materialism + credit = enslavement to our own self-deception. add that to the fact that workplace dissatisfaction and stress are the number one health problem for working adults and spending soon becomes your salvation. plastic will keep getting used for that distant "one day when i am doing what i really want to be doing with my life . . . " and the reverse is true as well. all the money in the world cannot give you the true abundance that comes only from living your soul. the distinction: where there is a need to hoard one's riches — there is wealth acquired by fear. where there is trust, generosity, and a desire to give to others / be of service to humanity present with wealth (remember socialist-capitalism?) — you can count on a life soulfully lived accompanying it. extreme abundance always comes with expressing the gifts of your soul in the way that only you can.

on the subject of depression, it is, in many instances, literally a *re*pression of the truth of our life's purpose. it is a living deadness that can easily cause most to misinterpret the signs in their life that are only crying out for them to go within and hear what their soul is screaming out for. instead, because they are petrified by these emotions, disconnected from themselves spiritually, and exhausted by the tirade of their minds, they just want to go numb. most doctors are powerless to treat (and sometimes even recognize) the root of their patients' state. so, they only treat the symptoms with a short–term fix via medication . . . if only it were short term. many people become addicted, never knowing where the actual root of the problem exists, as they become steadily more anesthetized to their life. what is happening neurologically is often intertwined with what is (or isn't) happening spiritually. known: you cannot treat the body as an entity separate from the soul . . . and especially in the case of spiritual desires in the self. they do not want us to fall into any deeper of a sleep . . . *they want us to wake up.*

>> you are tangled up in others and have forgotten what your heart once knew. <<

kabir

to honor your desires, you have to know what they are first.

do you ever find yourself eating when you want to be working out / having casual sex when you really want emotional intimacy / crying at a sappy movie when you really want to be meditating at home / working as an art buyer when you truly want to create art / reading ten new books at the same time when you are actually wanting to train for a triathlon / planning a wedding when you are not sure if you are ready to marry yourself, let alone someone else . . . ?

there are several aspects of the self that desire. each aspect is like an instrument in a symphony. when everyone is playing the wrong part (and, oh, baby, the oft–autocrat mind usually has to pick the tuba — a painful and unfortunate choice) then there is dissonance. it is torture enough to listen to, let alone live through. note: our brain is meant to be the computer, not the conductor of our lives. however, when each aspect is fed, nourished, and expressed, and playing its own part, there is incredibly beautiful music to be heard and to be lived.(!)

this requires the art of deep listening to the different aspects of the self. notice how this fragmentation is reflected back in the collective. connect.the.dots between where we are at war between head and heart in the individual, and where we are at war with, say, science (head) and religion (heart) in the world. where else do you see individual disconnection mirroring collective disconnection? (your choices are many.)

aspects of the self:

~physical   ~spiritual   ~emotional
~intellectual   ~sexual   ~creative

[note: no matter what . . . the flames of your soulfire can never go out. they can only dim, waiting for you to fan and feed them once again.]

>> desire, ask, believe, receive. <<
stella terrill mann

assignment:

feed the fire = feel the fire

a:
what is your absolute core **desire** in each aspect of your self?
go through all six, one by one, and explore what is it that you really want. i mean, really, underneath —
what you think you want . . . plumb the depths here and simplify it to its essence.

b:
for your journal:
when our true desires are not owned and expressed, they get re-routed, like a fireball, into other aspects
of our self. (and they often end up in the binge eating / partying category . . . sound at all familiar?) ask
yourself now: where have i turned my own power against myself by not knowing how to honor my true
desires? where have i given up on and silenced my true desires? (apply your new tool of self-compassion.
you will definitely need it.)

small steps carry us across the universe: make it a rule to honor your core desires by *acting* upon
them = instant guilt remover. + your courage will be rewarded in ways you cannot even imagine.
when you are out taking action on behalf of your self-fire (and as you are using the trusty guidance
from your daily self-connection), try chanting the mantra "ibelieveinmysoul — itrustinmysoul —
ibelieveinmysoul."

>> you can have anything you want if you want it desperately enough. you must want it with an exuberance
   that erupts through the skin and joins the energy that created the world. <<
sheila graham

i will tell u this . . . these are the words that kept me breathing the morning i went to meet dr. martin luther king, jr.'s partner and mentor. i told him that i had been called to begin a global movement for unity and that i needed his support. and he said "yes." get this: not only did i not pass out . . . but i also experienced the deepest soulfire-aliveness of my entire life that day. **when you have the courage to follow your soul, a feeling of rightness and bliss that can only be described as orgasmic will follow.** oh, yeah. what happens next is simply part o' the candyland adventure . . . the most important point is that you hear, honor, and express your core desires. they were given to you for a reason. *a divine reason.* it is not your job to know how it will all happen. (the how will come the clearer you become.) your only job to say "yes," to stay committed to the fire of your soul, and then just get ready to enjoy the ride . . .

c:
fasten your seatbelts . . . 'cause we're goin in. yep, it is time for some passion play.

1) slip into something a little more comfortable. 2) light a candle and set the mood with some music. 3) set a timer for three minutes (this will be a quickie unlike any other i promise you), and then, with several pieces of blank paper and your favorite pen in hand, answer these two questions with as many responses as you can in the three minutes. do not stop, do not judge, do not think about it. just go as fast as your little fingers can take you. ok: ready . . . set . . . breathe . . . **connect!**

what are you passionate about in life?
what is it that truly and deeply moves you?

go all out — from butterflies — to healthy contraception — to children being loved — to the abolition of american-apartheid — to men who honor women — to elderly people having parties celebrating their soul before they die — to silly movies — to dancing to a funky world music dj until you sweat . . . yeaah, ok. u get the idea.

>> get in the habit of noticing what you gravitate towards. <<
barbara sher

when finished, high-five yourself (ok, just clap once) and step away from your list for a minute. when you come back to it, slowly go through the list and circle the things that you feel resonate the most for you.

in wildness is the preservation of the world.   >> henry david thoreau

what are things you are *wildly* passionate about from your list?
when have you felt the most a-l-i-v-e?
what qualities of yourself were present in those moments?

revisit this exercise as many times as you want until you feel your final list nails it.
then, when you have your final oh-yes-that-is-it-list . . . you will understand that:

$$\downarrow$$

**the purpose of your soul
is its deepest desires = your self-fire**

no one can give you this,
and no one can *ever* take it away.

>> what you love is a sign from your higher self of what you are to do. <<
sanaya roman

self
fire

stage eight: manifestation — the union

we love because it's the only true adventure.

>> nikki giovanni

suggested soulfire soundtracks for this section:
<> *city of angels*: soundtrack   <> dinah washington: *blue gardenia: songs of love*
<> *susana baca*: (self-titled)   <> *when love speaks*: various artists
<> harry connick, jr: *to see you*   <> tracy chapman: *new beginning*

suggested soulfire fieldtrip destinations for this section:
<> whether you are single or coupled . . . take yourself on a date and end it parked somewhere overlooking the ocean or a lake and turn on the radio . . . let every love song be to you and from you. set your heart free.

it is in our interactions with other human beings that we have the opportunity to experience either the luminous reflection of our own soul, or the dark cavern of its disconnection. observe (and connect.the.dots) — the way that most couples interact is the way many nations interact with each other . . . warfare is a very popular way of relating it would seem. just as nations seek to (both overtly and covertly) exploit each other, we unconsciously objectify each other in relationships, seeking or demanding the lost parts of ourselves; coming together not in wholeness, but in need; not in freedom, but imprisonment. relationships have become an exchange of "i will commit to you if you can guarantee me the love i need." the commitment is based on need that the other person is expected and depended upon to fulfill. this is futile because you will never be able to love that person enough to fulfill what they are imploring you to provide. eventually, it will not be enough for them and that is a tragic day for all involved. this is a rapidly dying model of relationship proven by our divorce rate. the more we search for love outside of us, the more elusive and eventually impossible (not to mention exhausting) it is to find.

there is a secret to all of this . . . **we must find our own soul before we look for its soul-mate**. when you fall in love with your own soul, you will become what you have been searching for all over the planet. this is a major turning point where being alone is no longer scary and you truly *get it* that you already are the love you seek. you will stop looking and start living because you will finally be at peace within yourself. then, trust me. if and when it is time, you will attract, like radar, the mate of your dreams, because they will be a reflection of your own self-connection and aliveness. and, hidey-ho, you will certainly know it when they arrive! your first clue is that everything will feel very, very easy and strangely natural. (and how else will you know? well, because they will likely explode your heart, which then, of course, opens you to hearing more and more of your soul.) intense love relationships open us to our soul purpose like nothing else can. + ding-ding-ding: you will be with them because you want them to share in the journey of living your soul, *not because you need them to substitute for it.*

you will understand with a profound clarity that the desire for union is wholly within you. the rest is truly just icing on the cake. (please read this paragraph again. *especially* if you spend more time internet dating than you do sleeping. just put down the mouse and step slowly away from the computer. easy now. it is not a date you are looking for . . . it is your own self.)

where the old agreements of relationships were to stay the same to protect each others emotional needs . . . there is now a new model emerging that is one of great expansion and growth — of opening instead of possession. (remember our good friend jerry maguire: mr. "you complete me"?) well, where two halves used to make one whole for most relationships . . . now, two complete circles come together to form an infinity sign (looks like an eight sideways ∞).

this new model of relationship requires a very different kind of love triangle: Δ

>> to be at peace with ourselves we need to know ourselves. <<
caitlin matthews

enter the model of **the new 'power couple'** for the next millennium: the commitment that is shared is not between the needs of two people but to a third point = the joint commitment that each person has to living **and being accountable to** their own soul . . . which forms their relationship as they do this together. each person is committed to inspiring and supporting the other towards living their best life a.k.a. their soul's purpose. each person's fundamental commitment is to themselves first and the relationship second. fyi: this is where the perfect blend of autonomy and intimacy is found.

note: please allow me to clear up a vast misconception: this is not selfish but actually quite generous. the most solid way to love another is to understand you must love yourself first. until you are conscious of this, you will only be giving your intention-to-love to others (you will be giving that + a package of your expectations and projected needs = a typical relationship). when you are giving to you, you automatically have more love to give everyone else. not to mention — life becomes a whole lot easier when you get this because you will stop fighting to prove the world loves you.
+ you will be free to spread love in the world instead.

---

life is a journey into the love in yourself.
a relationship is meant to be the passenger on your plane = your companion,
not your pilot and air traffic control.

>> love is but the discovery of ourselves in others, and the delight in the recognition. <<
alexander smith

rewind: "selfishness," by definition, refers to the priority and care of the disconnected self. this is confusing, because you constantly hear of people who use that "i need to do this for myself" bit as an excuse for basically anything. and it can easily be a very manipulative action. the clearest way to discern if someone is acting on behalf of genuine self connection or from the disconnected self is if the choice is coming from either love or from fear. actions from fear are selfish. acting on behalf of the commitment to be accountable to your own soul is an act of love and self-full. (+ true self-connection is also evidenced by the presence of humility and a consideration of others). count on the knowledge that those who truly love you will understand and support actions taken on behalf of your commitment to honoring yourself.

this, in fact, is what the true meaning of friendship is all about.

an inspire soulfire decree = be audaciously self-full!

>> no one has measured, not even poets, how much the heart can hold. <<
zelda fitzgerald

recipe for bliss
a.k.a. the famous brown bag formula

let's just say you are someone single who really, and i mean, really wants a relationship.
in fact, you so desire this that until you meet that person, it almost (i said "almost")
feels like you are in a kind of a holding pattern of delayed gratification until they arrive . . .
(when is it my turn? why not me? where are all the good ____?) know that you
do not have to wait to meet that person to start experiencing what i call professional joy —
(you know, where folks start to demand all your secrets) and that, in fact, it is actually the other way around:

you will not find the relationship you truly desire until →
(and i don't mean the ol' "we went out, had a great time,
so i guess i'll see them again," i mean the *rock-your-world* relationships) . . .
until you have found your own soul's joy first!!

assignment:

so, here is how to start cooking with crisco:

1) preheat oven to 475 degrees (that would be you, o hot one)

2) now, what are the experiences you are craving in a relationship? for example:
   > fun dates   > travel   > deep everlasting love
   > affection   > deep everlasting love   > + hot, sensual, passionate intimacy
                                                      (+ any other qualities you desire to experience here)

>> there is only one blasphemy, and that is the refusal to experience joy. <<

paul rudnick

3) what are the essences at the core of these experiences?

> to use the above example . . . fun dates = spontaneity
affection = tenderness
travel = adventure / openness
deep everlasting love = connection to the heart

4) where are those qualities found within you? spontaneity = your zest for tasting the unknown
tenderness = being nurturing to yourself
openness = your willingness to learn
connection to the heart = your sense of compassion, etc.

5) what actions can you take to cultivate those qualities today?
zest for unknown = learn rock climbing
willingness to learn = take a salsa class
being nurturing to yourself = cook a great meal for one
sense of compassion = volunteer to tutor kids

you will find that applying this recipe is a way of living life. it is to become a love machine in the truest sense. what all of us desire most are experiences that open us to taste our delicious lives, not the box they came in. there are many different boxes that contain the same delight. follow me? remember this and become adept at being able to pinpoint the essence of your desires, create from them, and then . . . well, prepare for a life orgasm. (fyi: there is nothing more attractive than someone wildly and audaciously alive anyway.) + if you apply this concept in current relationships, not only does good lovin' taste even better, but the question of infidelity becomes something inane. you will truly understand that everything you need and desire you already have within you the tools to create it.

so, just bake for 30 minutes and let cool. then, bon appétit! **yum.**

>> to love oneself is the beginning of a life-long romance. <<
oscar wilde

117

when people get married today, most are forgetting the most important step: marrying themselves first! inner union precedes outer union. this is the foundation for every **real-ationship**. (remember, you are only in a relationship with yourself. your mate simply shares in it.) note: you are welcome to get married at any time without this step. it just means you are in store for one wild ride to self-discovery.

as a culture, we put all the emphasis on having the fairy tale wedding . . . and very little on the preceding one that is quite critical to the success of your actual marriage. is it any wonder that few marriages survive? and out of the ones that survive, that there are even fewer that contain any aliveness? (yikes.) like baking a cake, you cannot skip steps. *life will always return you to your own relationship with yourself.*

your journey into inner union is the most sacred marriage there is. so, what is it to be in union in yourself? it is to contain the balance of the two forces of the universe: the divine masculine and feminine energies. and every human being has both (although one's gender usually determines the primary energy). the degree of union in the individual is the degree they are connected to the essence of both energies in balance within themselves.

what is inner unity?
female and male divine energies unlock and come into balance:
the power of love + the power of creation
receiving + giving
being + doing
left brain + right brain
inner + outer
spiritual + physical
heaven + earth
=
union

>> relationships are only alive as the people engaging in them. <<
donald ardell

the union of the divine feminine and divine masculine energies comprise
the life force of the universe = spirit + form

the divine feminine

when connected to, the qualities are:

> receptive = magnetic energy
> heart centered groundedness
> honors emotion as sacred
> wisdom / grace / beauty
> compassion / tenderness
> trust
> intuition
> beingness / peaceful
> acceptance
> life energy / radiance
> conceiving
> *the power of love*

when disconnected:

> lives by analysis / in the head
> incessant quest for perfection
> numbs / silences emotions
> defensive / blaming / petty
> sexually dishonest / manipulative
> predatorial
> anxiety high / energy low
> relies on the advice of others
> a need to (be in) control
> compulsive caretaking

the divine masculine

when connected to, the qualities are:

> active energy = expressive energy
> soul–guided action in the world
> courage / presence of honor
> strength / protection
> directness in expression
> conviction
> abundant manifestation
> ease in doing / productive
> discipline
> clarity of vision
> bringing into form
> *the power of creation*

when disconnected:

> overwhelmed / exhausted
> fear / distrust
> alienated / hostile
> judgmental / bitter
> need for sexual conquest
> aloneness / fear of intimacy
> survival mode / competitive
> fear of dependence
> refuses to be controlled
> subjugation / destruction

>> the heart is the hub of all sacred places. go there and roam in it. <<
sri nityananda

with inner union, there is a deep synthesis of heart and soul. all of the other aspects of the self come into perfect balance around this core communion. when we speak of truly being power-full . . . **this** is the source. to awaken the universal life force of the divine feminine and masculine within us, we must begin to become more aware of the true faces of both divine energies outside of us, *not just one or the other*. the creative force of the universe has no gender and no race . . . it transcends definition or personification, although nearly every culture throughout history has attempted to make it their own — that really is quite impossible. we have inadvertently evolved into worshipping those whose lives were meant only to inspire us and to return us to the truth within us. may we, as a world, forgive ourselves for the *many times* we have tried to strip others of their own way to connect and replace / govern / "save"(!!?) them with our own. **this is the most arrogant and serious crime against humanity that could exist.** and let us not forget the category that the majority of us fall into: we who have nailed shut our own doors into deafening silence and have instead walked through someone else's door who claimed a superior connection to the divine. hear this. *there is no such thing.* the only thing you have ever lacked was your conscious cultivation of your own connection. take a moment and connect.the.dots here politically, for this has repeatedly occurred all over the world.

let us each remember that every single human being has equal access in the most sacred and profound sense. *your soul is your religion.* it really does not matter what name we give it . . . we may each have our own doors, but we are all still going to the same room.

the universal life force is like the core of the sun's fire, and every soul on the planet contains one of its rays . . . the more that you connect to your own soul . . . the more you are accessing the spiritual source of all creation.

for journaling — **godeep2theroot:** what is your relationship to the divine presence for you now? . . . this is a relationship that is the richest and most evolving part of our life if we allow it to be. how has it changed over the course of your life? how has it been affected by cultural conditioning? how does it affect your relationship to authority? this relationship is the most personal, cherished, mystical, and dimensional that we will ever know as human beings. it is the foundation of all our lives.

to know the soul of the one that dwells within you is to know the soul of all . . . this is to live knowing you are truly never alone.

>> every person should define for themselves their attitude towards this world and towards divinity. <<
leo tolstoy

the relationship you have to your own soul is the single most important relationship in your life. every other relationship is only an extension and reflection of this.

wherever we are in our relationship to ourselves will be reflected back to us in the people we meet and in our environment. (yes, our children and pets are included in this.)

the world is a precise mirror:

simply put, everyone reflects one of three things:
> who you were
> who you are
> who you are becoming.

every person contains the same spectrum of human possibility.

the people you admire and the people you detest are all your reflection of the relationship you have with yourself — when you are fully accepting of yourself, you can be fully accepting of and compassionate with others (even if you do not like them). you can observe anything in anyone, but where there is judgment, blame, a distressed or hostile reaction, there is a neon sign to your own shadow.

make a list of ten people you really admire and ten people you cannot stand.
have them all written down? good. now change all their names to your own.

what you hate in others is what you hate and deny in yourself. and what you truly admire and love in others are the qualities of your own self shining back to you. anything you react to intensely always contains a truth about yourself within it.

whom we love and whom we hate are our most powerful teachers.

>> if you judge people, you have no time to love them. <<
mother teresa

go2theroot:
a common myth of self-help circles: "those negative people"

enter any hotel conference room on a weekend where you find a group of people voluntarily locked up for 12 hours at a time, and you will likely hear this statement or something close to it: "we must cut negative people out of our lives! they are toxic and we must ruthlessly remove them or we are just accepting that we have no self-worth." (this is one of the many gems you will be given in between getting enrolled for the next seminar.)

let's bring the light of self-truth here, shall we?

actually, if you follow the above instructions, the people you have "ruthlessly cut out of your life" will only return . . . except this time with a different face and name.

a self-truth: cutting people out = holes. embracing the reflection = wholes.

when you can see with the eyes of love, truth, and compassion, you will see that this person is only reflecting a part of you that you have disowned. (for example: where you devalue yourself will be reflected by someone very cruel and critical in your life.) your focus needs to be on what they reflect in you, not how much of a yank they are (that is for them to deal with). remember, you drew them to you, my friend. **the true law of attraction in life is that your soul is a magnet** that draws everyone in your life to you to reflect and awaken who you are. every single person who comes into your life does so to bring you a gift. (a gift, *not* a lesson. key distinction. everyday is christmas, not halloween = gratitude, not fear.) therefore, when you forgive, honor, and integrate what that "negative" person reflects,

the said "toxic" (who is probably more wounded than toxic) person will disappear because they have nothing more to reflect or no buttons of yours to push anymore. such disconnected (my word for "toxic") people will just **self-select** right out of your life. it is that easy. (no dramatic phone calls required to 'break-up' with friends and family . . . sigh, the uglies are, oh, so unnecessary.) here is a concept: just let your relationships reveal themselves. (which they will anyway.) express the truth that you stand for, and then watch what happens . . . many will come as many will go. there is great wisdom in the understanding that life is a circle. know that people come in and out of our lives for one reason:
to teach us that love never leaves.

note: sometimes, who you are is most clearly evidenced by being around those *who you are not*. thank them heartily for the gift of awakening and then head for the hills. and let me tell you, there are few things sweeter than the relief this provides!! → some of the greatest awakenings and gifts of my life have come through this door. + bonus: the more you are connected to yourself, the more you will magnetize that reflection. of course, this creates space for people to come into your life who reflect the connection to the beauty of your soul. yaaay!!!

surround yourself with people who celebrate and inspire your soul.
life is too short to do otherwise.

>> there are as many ways to live and grow as there are people. our own ways are the only ways that should matter to us. <<
evelyn mandel

go2theroot: the beauty of death = a celebration of a soul fully alive on this earth

close your eyes and spend a few minutes connecting to your breath.
allow your body to feel firmly grounded and relaxed.
placing one hand on your heart,
and the other over your belly button as you deepen your breath even more . . .
allow it to slow down as you become centered.
when you are ready, begin to ask yourself this question:

visualize that you are 85 years old, and it is the last day of your life . . .

where are you?
how do you feel?
who have you become?
who is in your life?
what are the relationships in your life at that point?
what has been your experience of love?

what have you created with your life and what meaning does this have for you?
what has been the impact your life has had on the world?
how at peace do you feel with why you are here?
how connected do you feel to your soul?

what is the legacy you leave behind?

what else do you see?

memento mori =
if you remember that you must die, then you will remember that you must live

---

although most of humanity waits until they are dying to know their soul,
you do not have to.
this is the great secret of life.

---

living our soul with full aliveness allows us to understand and greet death
with a sense of peace, beauty, and gratitude.

>> it is only in the giving of oneself to others that we ever truly live. <<
ethel perry andrus

soulfire: the birth of wild aliveness

assignment:

in your soulfire journal:
fingerpaint the last sunset you would want to see
on the last day of your life . . .
what else would you want to do?

now go do it today

ponder the meaning of this: **this miraculous existence and impermanence of form
always makes the illumined ones dance and sing.** >> **hafiz**

* note: the above statement becomes especially significant and thought-provoking while watching
any episode of the phenom show *six feet under.*

~ play so that you may be serious.~   >> anacharsis in aristotle's *nicomachean ethics*

assignment:

wonder twin power . . . activate!
form of: a ridiculously epic weekend.

plan . . . then embark upon a soulfire adventure away by yourself (or, even better, with some partners in crime hip to what you are doing and whose souls are on fire, too); go somewhere fabulous for an entire weekend with your itinerary focused on one singular intention: **wild aliveness.**

ponder these three questions during your travels:
how does being wildly alive alter your perception of death?
how does being connected to your soul alter your meaning of life?
what is your signature aliveness motto? (mine is "spread love" thanx to mi corazon.)

create a scrapbook for you to fill with tangible evidence of the joy and incredible time i know u will have. as aristotle said: happiness depends upon ourselves. so, make this the most mythic and amazing weekend ever. (it is not so much what you do but how you will do it.) make it something that becomes such legend in your life that you shall always remember and break into a big stupid grin whenever you think of it. and, afterwards, if it appeals to the journalist in you, describe every juicy detail and escapade in your journal, especially those events where you nearly hyperventilated from laughing so hard.
that there is the badge of wild aliveness, my friend. consider yourself initiated.

the most sober and serious spiritual question one can ever ask in life is this:
got joy?

>> go outside to the fields . . . enjoy nature and the sunshine. <<
anne frank

selffire

stage nine: the delivery — true creativity

it is
our
divine right
to
create.

>> hildegard von bingen

suggested soulfire soundtracks and singles for this section:
<> sheila chandra: *zen kiss*   <> soulstance: *truth, simplicity, and love*
<> zero 7: *simple things*   <> k.d. lang: *all you can eat*
<> des'ree: *supernatural*   <> jon mayer: *your body is a wonderland* — *(acoustic/ep)*
<> creed: *with arms wide open / don't stop dancing (acoustic/ep)*

suggested soulfire fieldtrip destinations for this section:
<> library → research the life of your fave artist   <> visit a maternity ward
<> interview people re: sexuality and journal about it   <> have your first life-O!

sex. the very word makes us lower our voice. we either don't want to talk about it at all . . . or it is all we want to talk about it. yet, it is probably one of the most misunderstood things in life. how does something so beautiful get turned into so much madness? if you were an alien that landed here from another planet, you would most likely think that sex is a very dangerous thing. just look at some of its many conclusions → aids, std's, abortion as birth control, rape, prostitution, pedophilia, sexual abuse, pornography, contraception that often endangers half of the populace, teenagers dumping newborns in dumpsters, and frequently, birth as a medical condition. and this is after hundreds of years of improvement! we clearly need some sexual healing. so, how is all this in a book about the soul? don't be shocked — sexuality and spirituality are actually two sides of the same coin.

sexual energy is the core creative energy of the universe. as we just explored the qualities of the universal divine presence in the last section as yin / yang and masculine / feminine, we saw how these two energies form an entity where active + receptive together is the life force that creates everything in the universe. here is where it gets very interesting and often highly misunderstood. in our culture, we have split sexuality and spirituality off to be opposite entities, but in truth they are deeply merged. when these two forces are divided and conflicting in our culture, darkness occurs all over our society, (hence, the reason why sexuality and violence typically are depicted together — go2theroot here, folks.) however, when they are united, there are great amounts of healing and light for one and for all.

the artist inside is where passion resides.

sexuality is the portal to the spiritual: our sexuality actually contains our divine nature, because sex is our own individual expression of the universal life force creating with us and through us. it is our literal power of creation — for a new life — or for the essence of our own. it is the doorway to true power as natural and beautiful, for when you connect to the meaning of this energy — you can use this power / energy and carry it over to create anything in the world / anywhere in your life. note: here is the catch — most people have a thick blanket of guilt and / or disconnect from their own sexual nature. where there was once, very naturally, innocence from the moment you were born and into your early childhood, you now have the cultural inheritance of centuries of shame. just think of how you felt naked as a child contrasted with how you feel naked today. where is the pleasure in this now? where is the joy and wonder of your own sexuality now?

underneath it all,
you're **naked.**

>> kenneth cole,
from a billboard on sunsetstrip, hollywood, california

amazingly, how you treat your sexuality actually affects your whole life — if you honor your sexuality as a sacred gift, then you will choose to express it in ways that honor its awesome power of creating life and that honors your own life as well. you will enjoy it immensely and express it in a way of deep love and respect as a part of the circle of life — whether you ever choose to use it to create life or not; and whether you choose to partner with the same or different sex, the power and the possibility is the same in your expression of love and ecstasy. you will experience a purity and a union in yourself that is *truly* divine. it is something you will enjoy not as a means to an end, but an end itself — whether you are alone or with a partner, the celebration of your sexuality is the same. you will celebrate the fact that there is a soul within your body so that when you make love (literally) your soul is present, too. there are few things more sexy in a man or woman than this.

the power of creation is the power of love

on the other hand, if you are unconsciously ashamed of your sexuality as dirty (are you a bad girl or a good girl?), you will have an unconscious relationship with your sexuality and your power of creation. you will constantly be at war with your body and conflicted, afraid, and distrusting of its desires (no, i mean "yes!" yes, i mean "no!"). affairs and one-night stands are things that somehow just, uh, happen. (hey, you are in control, right?) you will want to have sex with someone because you want only their body, not their heart, soul or anything else (which will still be present anyway). the words *getting laid, pussy, cock* will be used indiscriminately with no comprehension of how much they dishonor the one who is speaking them. you will use your sexuality as a tool for manipulation to get what it is that you want, whether that is a relationship, a release of pent–up emotion, or a baby. (not to mention the effect disconnected sex has on the actual conception, for it does. the degree of consciousness present at conception has great impact. connect.the.dots, *please*. the proliferation of so many 'problem children' is hardly random.)

>> in order to create there must be a dynamic force, and what force is more potent than love? <<
igor stravinsky

you will not understand that when you have sex with someone, you are first and foremost scientifically experiencing a very large transference of energy — what the other is giving, you will receive and vice versa. (especially as a woman — remember your physiology and feminine essence is to receive. is his energy really something you want to receive??) still, you will think it is just casual sex (when energetically, there is actually no such thing) . . . until, say, you catch a disease or until a pregnancy results. then you will have an overwhelming responsibility that demands immediate intimacy (and all from the person whose last name you still do not know). it is all yours to contend with, for it is no small thing to trifle with a soul. ignorance is not as blissful as we think.

why be so on fire about all this? because the more disconnected we are from ourselves, *especially* sexually, the more disconnected we become from each other. and, frankly, the amount of darkness in the world demands that the silence be broken and the possibility be explored of how self-connected sexuality brings much light . . . to ourselves and to each other.
this happens to be a huge door for our future evolution of the human condition.

when we are connected to our spiritual center, we are also connected to the fact that our sexuality is sacred. you still have absolute freedom with how / where / why you choose to express it; however, your consciousness on what sex is just starts to really shift. you begin to understand that your sexuality is nothing to control, but instead, something to honor. as with everything we fear (yes, many of us are deeply afraid of the power within our own sexuality), we try desperately to control it only to find out we will eventually be spanked (no pun intended).

as you begin to open to this awesome power and understand how that life force — your own personal supply of the universal power of creation — is actually at the heart of everything you create and available to you . . . your entire life now falls under the scope of creativity because you become aware that this power of creation extends out from your soul to every single piece of your life. you begin to be the creator, the author, the artist of your life in every way — from the relationships you seek to create in your life, to your life's work — to the way you parent. and you begin to realize the sacred privilege your body contains and celebrate it instead of hide it. and, fyi, the more you tune into this, the stronger your sex drive becomes. **yowza.** our sexuality is inexorably united with our creativity, power, and spirituality. and the unfolding of this can truly be one of the most beautiful things in life.

in our modern culture, the glaring absence of this is can be found in women (if you are a man, please keep reading because this is equally vital for you to understand). we have a predominantly adversarial role to our own bodies, the way they look "or should look" and the things that our bodies do inspire more "eews!" than "aahs!" (refer to stage four). the very aspects that impart women with an immediate connection to their sacred roots and power are the aspects most denigrated. example: the menstrual cycle. **fact: this is our connection to the rhythm of all of life as it lives within our own body.** every 29 days or so we undergo an intense cycle of birth and death. it is now known medical knowledge (thank you, thank you, dr. christiane northrup) that in the days immediately preceding a woman's cycle is when she is at the height of her intuitive powers and most clearly tapped into the spiritual realm. emotions become crystal clear. this is when you feel the truth about your life most immediately and deeply, and the information encoded here will inform you in ways nothing else can about the expression of your own true self and life. as a woman, it is natural that we be connected to our own cycles as the portal to creation within us and around us. the body truly is the doorway to the soul, and for women, this is true in a very compelling way.

>> lying, walking, sitting in the sun, she felt herself ripening and coloring. <<
meridel le sueur

---
our sacred responsibility is to give birth to our own life
---

it would follow that in a culture where **success for a woman = be a man in drag,** that our menstrual cycle would be viewed as something vile. (fyi: "be a man in drag" was a phrase i had proudly coined for myself as a young woman. gee, can you tell who was my first and most difficult / hardheaded / disconnected client ever? just take a wild guess.) + who can forget the ol' "i don't trust anything that bleeds for 7 days but doesn't die" joke? well, it is no longer funny and it actually never was. women have ingested this shame about themselves, and, as a result, the degree of disconnect here very often shows up as writing on the wall, better known as pms and / or pmdd — premenstrual dysphoric disorder; something that is intensely far and beyond the natural processes of the body. this is but one of the many examples of "disorders" that stems from this same numbness from the wisdom and power within the body of woman.

(many) female disorders = (many) disconnected females.
much compassion, gentleness, and awakening are needed in the body of women.

additionally, this does not include the equally foreign dimension that the honoring of the menstrual cycle takes us to: **fertility.** most women have a very defunct relationship with this. contraception is a headache, to say the very least. we are never taught that in actuality, men are more fertile than women. yes, that is correct. men are fertile everyday of the year and women are generally fertile only three to seven days a month.

>> most people die before they are fully born. creativeness means to be born before one dies. <<
erich fromm

it is a myth that fertility is the sole jurisdiction of women. therefore, when you honor your cycle (and this applies to men and women), you naturally honor your fertility and your power of creation; and subsequently become much more in tune with your own body. men and women who understand this will be in awe of each other's fertility biology. this is so imperative for men for many reasons — including, but not limited to: how many men have felt completely victimized and powerless when the very last thing they want is to be the father of a baby but somehow got a women pregnant because they had no idea about the fertility phases of a woman's body? both men and women need and deserve to know this(!) before they have intercourse if they have zero intention of having a pregnancy result.

knowledge is power.

for women, this understanding would cause us to reevaluate a lot of things we put into our bodies that turn its natural brilliance into chaos. the wisdom of our body is a very finely tuned instrument that can be turned upside down with the wrong choices. (try asking your body what it wants before you put something in it. this goes for food, drug, or anything / *anyone* for that matter.) go2theroot → menstrual cramps are often the way our bodies direct our attention to where we are most shut off from ourselves. cramps are not to be cured but heard(!).

for women, our self-connection to the trinity of heart + soul + womb is directly linked to our bodies' well-being and optimal functioning.

this entire conversation applies to the question of infertility as well; there is a direct spiritual component linked to a couple's ability to conceive. the consciousness and intention of both people comprise the first gateway a soul enters through. their bodies simply follow their lead. i have seen many fertility success stories result from this knowledge and its implementation. as you can imagine, this work transforms relationships too. this is an emerging field that will explode as people integrate this knowledge into their own lives.

>> curiosity, awe, and wonder must be kept alive. <<
eleanor roosevelt

what follows, of course, is that when women do become pregnant, this can become the most spiritually wondrous time in all of their lives. and the way we will treat pregnancy and the birthing process will finally reflect that someday soon. the birthing environment plays a pivotal role in the birthing experience, as does the consciousness and state of being in the mother, as well as the father. often, the most powerful and healthy parents are those who have already given birth to their own life before they endeavor to create another. it takes a village = we must urgently support people in the socially imperative role of conscious parenting: self-connection is crucial to effective parenting because you cannot teach love . . . *you must be it.*

how sexuality, pregnancy, birthing, and women's bodies are culturally perceived has a profound political counterpoint. the consciousness of a culture can always be clearly assessed by its corresponding valuation of the women within it. as women literally em-body the intersection of the physical and spiritual worlds, they truly possess a very powerful role at this point in history where these two worlds now yearn to unite as one. as women awaken and rise, they pave the way for the rest of the world as a living example of unity between the spiritual and physical realms that are so critically needed in our current global political condition. women symbolize *the sacred power of life.* as women remember this, their presence is a beacon of illumination in a world where it is numbly forgotten that every human life is truly sacred. i do not consider my position to be one of a feminist, but instead as one of a (self-defined) womanist = she who honors and celebrates the power and beauty of the feminine. for the last several thousand years, the feminine, as an energy, has been historically devalued, denigrated, and whored. and it has been reflected all across the face of our planet. where her energy is most tragically devoid is where there is the most warfare (example: the middle east). it is time for her energy to awaken in all of us. the body of a woman is the body of the earth, and she has suffered in silence for far too long. and yet, she is not the only one. men suffer equally in their own silence and confusion, for this is about men just as much as it is about women.

>> men are not the enemy. the real enemy is women's denigration of themselves. <<
betty friedan

it is time men stop being villainized for everything wrong in the world from infidelity to global warming. they are not the enemy. and men are so tired of having to be what women alternately demand of them to be and / or resent them for being — instead of just allowing and appreciating them for expressing simply who they are.

and wow . . . when men are that, it is a vision more glorious than a thousand sunsets to witness a man who lives by honor, wisdom, and an open heart that shines with the radiance of love and the humility of greatness. (i swoon just writing that as there as so many phenomenal men in the world . . . and a bunch of them happen to surround and inspire me. how i love being me.)

* men, please pay close attention to these pages. men and women are called to inspire and support one another in bringing the next . . . and there is a new breed of woman looking for you to recognize her. understand the road she travels and you will better understand your own. remember, a true revolution includes both sexes and all nations.

>> i paint my own reality. <<

frida kahlo

let us be clear on what is the position of a **womanist** —
it is to stand for union.
clearly it serves no one to swing from one end of the pendulum to the other.
our world has already seen both matrifocal and patrifocal societies,
and neither is now applicable for the needs of the modern human condition.
again, we are urgently required to create a new way = the middle way:
one that is the synthesis of the truth and power contained within each of these.
the joining of the beauty in both is the doorway to the future of our world.

let us welcome the dawn as we each remember who we are.

men and women are redefining themselves in equally transformative measures.
and we need each other as deeply as the sun needs the moon.

as we awaken to the true feminine *and* masculine energy in ourselves,
we awaken it in the world.
as men and women, let us, finally, celebrate love together.

assignment:

a:

recall the best sex you have ever had. (ok, or wanted to have.) what is your recipe for making fabulous love? really, what are the things you consider most important sexually — what qualities and ingredients comprise great sex for you?

list them by the quality, example:
connection
communication
vulnerability
etc. . . .
surprise! this is your own personal recipe for making love to life!!!
your relationship to your sexuality is at the heart of your relationship to life.

when you awaken one, you awaken the other.

observe: when you feel fully alive, you feel fully sexual. and the opposite applies:
if you are feeling "sexually dysfunctional" = nada aliveness.
the key to sauciness is not about solving your orgasm problemo.
the key is in realizing you are working on having the wrong kind.
when you are having life orgasms . . . then, trust me, the other kind will follow.

so, go get cooking!!!
a passion for life is one of the most beautiful gifts you can give the world.
and, hey, you will glow, too.

>> i am curled by the wind, painted by the sun. <<
julia de burgos

when you are turned on to your own sacred life force, you are turned on to life.

your spirituality melds with your sexuality to bring an exquisite synthesis of juicy,
passionate aliveness. pleasure and sensuality take on a whole new dimension that informs how you
walk through the world. you won't just smell the flowers anymore. you will want to touch them, too.
being sexy becomes less and less about someone else watching and more and more about how you
experience and savor your life, how open you are to
yourself, and how much you are willing to let go and taste the ecstasy
that lives at the center of who you are.

this is divine rapture indeed(!)
connect to your aliveness = **have multiple life orgasms**

it is a myth that sacred sexuality equates solely to incense, chanting, and meditation alone. it does,
however, mean embracing an openness and freedom to honoring the expression of the full spectrum
of who you are . . . the primal, wild, playful, ravenously insatiable sides included. soul and body,
spiritual and material, all long to be united as one. we are far too accustomed to splitting our
desires into either the spiritual or the physical, into either the primal or the pure, when in truth
this cannot be done. this can only result in frustration and judgment on our own sexual expression.
in truth, the two worlds are intimately intertwined. realize this and not only will you stop fighting
your desires, you will trust them and immensely enjoy their exploration.
this is the doorway to true ecstasy. come on in, a world of pleasure awaits you.

you will never stop discovering new ways to feel aliveness
through exploring and honoring your sexuality.

>> let the beauty we love be what we do. <<
rumi

>one is not born, but rather becomes a woman.

>> simone de beauvoir

b:

for women → celebrate the circle of life as it lives in you
the following is a ritual that, if done every month, it will astound you by how much it opens you to release and create in your own life . . .

1) make a special journal soul-ly for your cycle, and then begin the following tradition that honors both the dark and the light:

<> every month, right before your cycle begins, take a day / evening / hour (as your life permits) to draw your energy in and just be quiet . . . in silence is power. then, use music to open you. your soundtrack here may range from (for darkness theme) nine inch nails, alannis morrisette, rage against the machine; to (light theme) opera, jazz, piano concertos, etc. the time right before your cycle begins is known as **the darkness**: make a list of all the qualities + ways of being + ways of living that want to be released and let go of. what wants to die out of your life? really tell yourself the truth here, my sisters. go into the dark and feel whatever it is you must be freed of. when you are through, dispose of your list accordingly. then . . .

<> on the first day of your cycle = **the dawn**: start a new page of what wants to be created and given birth to in your life *right now* . . . please use crayons ~ glitter ~ feathers if u are so inspired to. then meditate with one hand over your womb and one hand over your heart affirming that it is so and that you trust that the desires of your soul and heart will be served. for they will. connect to your breath and see them link into one circle of light as you breathe. as you do this breath, allow your womb to metaphorically birth these desires. feel the peace that this brings in your body . . . for it is like none other.

start to chart your cycle and learn when you are most fertile and how that corresponds
to your cycles of creativity because it does.

+ wherever you are in the seasons of your life as a woman, the rhythms of your changing cycles
will always be your strongest guides.

how you treat your cycle is how you treat your womanhood.
your blood is holy and sacred and so are you.

2) honor the feminine = celebrate real birth-days.
start a tradition (for men and women): every year on the day of your birth, write your mom a card
or a letter thanking her for giving you life. if you can, celebrate with her. the meaning of this to your
mother is unimaginable. whatever relationship you have with her, this will exponentially open it.
(for women) to honor our own womanhood, we must come to peace with and honor our mothers.
our relationship to our mothers is at the heart of understanding ourselves.
(thank you, nancy, for inspiring this.)

>> i hear the singing of the lives of women, the clear mystery, the offering, and the pride. <<
muriel rukeyser

**w
o
m
a
n
i
s
t**

are u a womanist?

a womanist is power-full. she is wildly alive.
she is filled with love. she celebrates the beauty of her own self, as well as the beauty
of other women *and* men. she is a goddess, a warrior, and a queen . . . and is sometimes
spotted running barefoot in the rain. she is fearless and grounded. she is a woman
on fire **and** a woman at peace. she is accountable to her own soul = she is a walking billboard
for self-truth. she is grateful to the many women and ancestors whose shoulders she stands
upon who have paved the way for her. she is both a visionary and a fierce realist.
she lives devoted to the truth in her life and in the world and takes a stand politically
for issues that impel her courage. her heart is wide open, and she loves freely.
she radiates the power of compassion and grace. she has life orgasms. lots of them.
(note: and lots of the other kind, too. but they kind of just follow when u are having
the big life-O kind.) of course, she is sensual and saucy, but she is also deeply honoring
of her own body and her sexuality. she has come home unto herself. and she has a
reeelly good time doing it. there is nothing she is waiting for. she does have it all . . .
all of herself and her life shows it. she is abundant. she is surrounded by those who adore
and cherish her, beginning with herself. she has nothing to prove, no one to blame,
and no war to wage . . . she does, however, have a lot to express. (though she does not
need your permission to express it.) her emotions are sacred and provide her
with great wisdom and guidance. she lives with fab-u-licious style and a wild sense of joy,
for a womanist is truly in love with life.

**she is a woman who sings the song of her soul
and she lights up and (effortlessly) changes the world because of it.**

so, how do you know if you are a womanist?
grab your mahnolo's (or hiking boots as the case may be)
and let's find out, shall we?

1) when you are naked, do you usually:
   a. spread on glitter body paint, turn on your blue light, and dance throughout your house.
   b. close the curtains, and, using at least four mirrors, inspect what you would look like walking away from your pretend boyfriend while naked.
   c. pinch at pieces of your flesh imagining what you would look like without them.
   d. put on clothes as fast as your hands will go.

2) when you are home for holiday family gatherings, do you:
   a. take this as an opportunity to connect and give love.
   b. play everyone's favorite family game of "find the love."
   c. talk as little as possible. oh, except when you get to the topic of your new job, and how much they like you, and how much money you are making.
   d. wear a disguise and make friends with any and all delivery personnel who enter your house. your odds are better there.

3) when you are with your hottie lover, the following is true:
   a. it's all about ravaging them and making a love sandwich . . . check back in 12 hours.
   b. very slow to initiate, but if you get up the courage then it's on like donkey kong! you are a freak in the best possible sense of the word.
   c. get up in the morning and put a little make–up on and then get back in bed and breathe heavy . . . waiting for them to catch on.
   d. get all dolled–up and then get in bed and lie there like a cold, dead fish (which is 50% due to you have no idea what to do and to the 50% belief this is what women are supposed to do).

4) the meaning of sex for you is:

   a. a sacred act where you can connect with the soul of another. it is the heart of your spiritual center and is a place of purity, ecstasy, and joy. it is the power of creation and you honor it in yourself.

   b. an expression of love, and honesty, and vulnerability.

   c. it has been too long to remember, but in the meantime you take your pleasure into your own hands (punctuated by big grin).

   d. you don't really like sex. it is dirty and you always feel ashamed. besides, what if your mother should call during it?

5) what is your definition of beauty?

   a. **shameless radiance.** you know and express that beauty comes from within, *and* you love to celebrate and share with the world your outer beauty, too.

   b. truth is beauty and beauty is truth. hmmm . . . you take that to mean wear as little make up as possible. being beautiful is not easy, but you work at it.

   c. beauty is a luxury, but you also see it as a realistic necessity. you never leave the house without your face on and a good padded bra . . . you get treated better that way. you secretly fear the fate of ever being "the ugly woman."

   d. bo*toxin* sounds like a scary thing — but hey if it can keep ya looking good, then bring that botchulism on! asap. (hey, can you buy some extra and inject yourself at home?)

6) what does age mean to you?
   a. increased opportunity for wisdom. the time to celebrate the circle of life completing itself through your journey of life. time to mentor, too.
   b. absolute freedom to be and enjoy everything you have created in your life.
   c. you hope and you pray you won't be an old maid and spend your last years alone.
   d. that they take you out in a field and leave you there when you start to drool.

7) what is your definition of power?
   a. living your soul and being of service to humanity.
   b. knowing who you are and expressing it in the world.
   c. to be the hottest woman at your 20–year high school reunion.
   d. being able to make everyone you don't like kiss up to you because you will be rich and famous. so there.

8) what is the objective of a real-ationship?
   a. to inspire and support each other, to live out your soulfire together, and bring love to the world.
   b. to have a good time together and not fight.
   c. to have someone take care of you so you are not alone.
   d. to not break–up and to get as much free stuff as possible.

w
o
m
a
n
i
s
t

if you answered all a's = you are a **womanist**

dang! you better start throwing womanist parties! you are a born leader in that you know your soul and your heart are the leader of your life. thank the women <u>and</u> men who have inspired your own ascent to greatness. you inspire all of us.

all b's = you are a **woma or wow**

high five yourself because you are well on your way to understanding the greatest power in life is to be found within your own self . . . and for women: in her own womb. you have made your own way in a world that gives little example of how to marry true power and sexuality. take a bath and reflect. smile at where you have come from and rejoice at where you are going.

all c's = you are a **wom or womb (womanist in becoming)**

take a deep breath and just ask yourself: where did my examples of what a woman is and what she can become originate from? whose definition of a woman am i living? what is my own? it is time to ask that question of yourself and become your own answer.

all d's = you are a **wo, or actually a whoa**

if you are waiting for me to yell at you to "get real," you can keep on waiting. you are skilled enough at your own shame game, sister! you do, however, need *to get connected* to yourself. as in quick. code red. stat. pronto. quicko. urgent-o. like right now, today. unless of course, you choose never to look at who you are and just stay bitter at the world for being unfulfilled instead. this is a very popular choice in our culture; however, it does not provide a very fruitful result. remember — not choosing is a choice, too.

life on the planet is born of woman. >> adrienne rich

the education and empowerment of women throughout the world cannot fail to result
in a more caring, tolerant, just, and peaceful life for all.
>> aung san suu kyi / nobel peace prize laureate leader of burma's democracy movement

please note: we acknowledge the incredible work and progress achieved by those working in the field of 'womanism.'
the word *womanist* was also used by the esteemed alice walker in the early 1970s to denote the experience of being a feminist
of african american descent. as introduced in this book, the soulfire definition of womanist is one for all women around
the world to claim as their universal anthem of power, honoring, and celebration. our voice is one. *may we raise it together.*

self fire

the birth of wild aliveness

whatever the soul knows,
it cannot fail to obtain.

>> margaret fuller

suggested soulfire soundtracks for this section:
<> diana ross: *i'm coming out!!!*   <> chaka khan: *this is my night*
<> india.arie: *strength, courage, and wisdom*   <> peter gabriel: *in your eyes*
<> ani di franco: *joyful girl*   <> donny hathaway: *sack full of dreams*
<> nuyorican soul: *you can do it baby*   <> u2: *beautiful day*
<> fun da mental: *ja sha taan* (transglobal underground karachi mix)

suggested soulfire fieldtrip destination for this section:
<> there is only one place to visit → go into your closet. stay there. a long time. look around. imagine spending your entire life there with no one ever knowing you, or hearing you, or what you have to say. then, when you have had just about all you can take . . . fling that door open, and hurl yourself out into the sunshine. now, don't you feel a whole lot better? good, because now you know exactly what your soul needs from you . . . to come out of the closet.

free your soul, and your life will follow.

is it really the end already? yep, you are so quick! you already guessed it.
indeed, it is only the very beginning . . .

as you awaken more and more to your soul, you are sure to know this:
you are always just beginning to know it. it is constantly, every moment,
evolving and unfolding beyond comprehension. like your fingerprint,
your own soul has an extraordinarily unique design that will never be repeated again
in history. never. (do you know how precious you are???) and not only that — it will also never end —
it is infinite as it stretches through all eternity, past-future-present. this is why it has everything
you could ever need within it — because it is connected, like a hologram, to everything else in the universe.

your soul contains the circle of life.

the soul's journey can be simplified into one sentence:
it is here to experience itself.
the deepest desire of every soul is allways love =
its own particular brand of love it came here to give and receive in this world
is the only thing it really wants from you.

this lives at the core of who you are and who you came to be in this life.

when you are connected to what qualities this is (and isn't) for you, then decisions like whom you will marry (if you will marry), what your life's work is, what you will choose to study, what path your life will take, and, in essence, why you will truly live — will already be essentially shown to you.
your job is simply this: to be willing to follow where you are guided to go.
it really is the grandest adventure imaginable.

---

the ultimate drug:
want to have the time of your life?
get high on self-truth

>> no bird soars too high if he soars with his own wings. <<
william blake

to live the joy of your soul
is to live an unmistakable life . . .
so, how can you spot someone who is living some soul joy?
simply observe: they will always shine very, very
b r i g h t l y

each one of us holds a critical piece, inside our soul, of what the world needs to complete this puzzle of creating a new possibility for the human condition now. and it is there waiting for every single human being on the planet. one must only awaken to it. no matter what your calling is, every single person has something extremely important to contribute. we have this wacky idea that the purpose of our soul is something we need to figure out and go do — like be an astronaut, or a famous dancer, or save the whales — today! this is a big fat hairy lie perpetrated to keep people paralyzed by inaction for fear of doing the wrong thing and messing it all up for good. know this, my beautiful friend . . . you can never mess it up because in truth, you can never ever fail your soul. its purpose is not a fixed role or destination you are supposed to assume — its purpose is to experience its own essence everyday of your life. in your walking, talking, breathing, and creating . . . if the essence of your soul is here to bring laughter and mirth, for example, then you don't have to move to los angeles and be a stand-up comedian to make good on your purpose! you can work at the post office cracking up the grumpy people in line and parent two darling children and be completely fulfilled.

there is nothing to wait for to begin living this joy.
it starts right n-o-w.

>> to know what you prefer instead of humbly saying amen to what the world tells you you ought to prefer,
is to have kept your soul alive. <<
robert louis stevenson

it is never too late or too early to begin this process. it is for whenever you are ready to choose it and say "yes" to who you truly are. you are the only one who can ever open to the depth of this ecstasy or to be the one to deny it. and you are the only one to truly reap the reward or feel its absence. whether you are fighting your true purpose in this life or whether you are celebrating the adventure of its unfoldment . . . it will always be revealed to you in the quiet moments of your life.

there is no faking this. *you will always know.*

the truth is a fire, and the more you fuel it, the stronger it will burn within you and illuminate your entire life. connect to your soulfire and feel the joy. *you know* you want to . . . (and really, who wouldn't?) everyday is a new day to keep saying "yes." otherwise, your soul will be hanging out waiting for you to wake up again and catch on to the grand and radiant purpose of why it is you were ever born to begin with. as you understand this and live it, life becomes quite simple actually. in time it will even become automatic pilot. the more you connect to your soul = the more you create from it = the more you experience your soul = the more wildly alive you become. sound good? that's because it is.

there is only one thing you must make sure you remember: *relax*. there is no spazzing out required here. you cannot self-sabotage the purpose of your soul, not even if you tried. actually, the only thing you can do is delay it. and that is more painful than anything else anyway. and, for the record, your soul is much stronger than anything your disconnection could ever dish out. you must only be willing to listen, and then, before you know it, a life that exceeds even your wildest dreams begins. like toucan sam, the soul always knows. **just follow your aliveness.** and then, have the courage to know that there really is nothing more important in life.

as you become increasingly aligned and more intimate in your self-connection,
you will soon realize there is no greater euphoria than living the fire of your soul.

it begins to feel like you have found out the greatest secret in the world and, well, you have.
the passion is completely infectious. and . . . it is real.

as they say, once you go soulfire, you never go back.

(+ your final assignment should give you something to knock it out of the park with.)

---

you are not your race
you are not your religion
you are not your gender

you are your soul

get to know it.

>> life is a promise, fulfill it. <<
mother teresa

final assignment:

a very special meditation — soul visioning

a:
> take about 15–20 minutes for this

> lie down somewhere comfortable
  [and you can either tape this or have someone you absolutely trust read it to you]

begin by feeling yourself lying upon a bed of warm sand that is covered with plush rose petals . . . the texture underneath your skin is very gentle and restful. the sun feels warm upon your face. you hear waves crashing and a gentle breeze blowing and there is a very peaceful silence surrounding you. as you lie there, you know exactly where you are.

you are on the island of the temple of your soul.

you gently feel yourself sit up, and as you begin to look around you, you see that i am walking towards you. i greet you with a big smile, take your hand, and help you rise. today is your day, and we both know it.

as you look in the distance, you notice there are no longer any of your old familiar dragons from your past anywhere around. in fact, the only thing in view is a glowing temple in a forest at the center of the island. you take a cleansing deep breath, and now, we begin to slowly walk into the forest together. in silence, you start to feel your footsteps match the rhythm of your breath . . . (pause). what do you notice as we prepare to enter this enchanted and lush forest?

as we get closer and closer to the temple, there is a strong fragrance of a certain kind of flower growing along our pathway . . . what kind of flowers are they? breathe in their deep fragrance . . . allow the scent to gently guide you to finding the temple . . . you feel yourself drawing closer and closer to it . . .

and then . . . *there it is.*

as we walk up to the door of this beautiful mystical temple, we stop in awe. it is truly magnificent. let yourself take a moment to examine its great majesty. (pause) as you look at the temple door, i turn to look into your eyes and you hear my voice say, "this is where my road ends and yours begins, for you no longer need me beside you. today you are to meet your greatest guide. it is time for me to say goodbye." and with that i squeeze your hand and disappear. you feel a warmth around your heart and know that i have not gone.
i am still with you, only now i am within you.

you feel a deep calm at this and feel yourself smiling as you turn to open the temple doors. as you walk in, everything feels oddly familiar here. the fragrance of those same flowers are strong as you enter. there is a very distinct and unusual energy of a sort of silent quality of joy you begin to notice inside the temple . . . it feels very palpable . . . like a heartbeat literally pulsing a sensation of serenity around you. just then, you hear someone calling your name to come in — you know they have been expecting you. the voice is very gentle and kind, and you feel a rush of anticipation as you walk through the doors and into the temple. what do you see inside the temple?

you enter one large room, and in the center of it are some pillows on the floor and some candles that are lit around it. you go in and sit down in the center.

as you do, you hear footsteps approaching you and feel a very bright light begin to emanate from under the doorway at the front of the room. you are aware that you are about to meet *an image of* your actualized soul. you are very jubilant but strangely relaxed at the same time. breathing slowly now, the door begins to slowly open, and into the room enters a stunningly radiant being . . .

allow yourself to take in every detail of their appearance, mannerisms, clothing, gaze . . .
what else are you feeling right now?

they introduce themselves and tell you what their name is. (fyi — it may be your own or another, possibly even from another language or time. it is common to time travel during this meditation.)

listen deeply to their voice and let it imprint itself deep within you. the voice is very distinct and transcends gender. it is very clear, loving, and extremely powerful. it is familiar to you.
they tell you how very happy they are to see you and that they have brought you a gift and they give it to you now. (what is it?)

they sit down in front of you and slowly begin to speak again.
      they tell you that they have brought a message for you . . .
            you listen to all they have to say now (pause for a couple of minutes).
                they ask you if you have any questions and you say "yes":
                    you ask, "what is it that you would have me know right now?"
                        again, you sit and listen to their response (within yourself).

"what is the essence of my soul here in this life?" (pause again / listen within)
when they are finished, you present to them a gift from you . . . they tell you it is time for you to go now . . . then they you tell you that you never have to say goodbye because they are allways with you. all you must ever do is call upon them for guidance. you now embrace one another and you notice that you are filled with a very, very deep sense of relief and comfort and a blissful feeling of what it is to finally come home into the temple of your soul. you stay alone in the temple for awhile and allow yourself to revel in what just happened, knowing that this rare experience is one that very few people have ever had throughout history . . . a sense of gratitude washes over you that this extraordinary privilege is yours. what else are you now feeling?

feel yourself begin to walk out of the room and to the back of the temple. you see a big golden door and open it. there are stairs. you climb them swiftly as they take you to the roof of the temple. on the roof, a helicopter awaits you. a certain quality of wild aliveness is starting to surge through your body . . . do you feel like skipping or perhaps you feel like walking very slowly? notice how you feel right now. you begin to walk with great conviction towards the helicopter and then climb in. you are ready to return. you close your eyes . . . you can feel yourself floating up, up, up, and through the sky . . . (pause) back over the ocean until you feel yourself being returned to right here and right now. connecting to your breath now you feel yourself slowly begin to wiggle your fingers, then your toes until you are now completely back in this room and when you are ready, slowly and gently opening your eyes . . . taking as much time as you need. welcome back, adventurer! *you are now truly home.*

journal everything you can remember.
repeat this as often as needed, and begin your own dialogue.

this is the place of your most profound guidance and inspiration for
the rest of your time on earth . . . travel back here as often as you like.
this relationship and the image you will be shown will continue to change and evolve
through your life as long as you keep opening the door to it!

the more you cultivate this relationship, the more it will infuse and inform each moment of your life.
after a while, you will find this connection to be like oxygen.

**= your soul is your greatest inspiration and guide.
trust this, for it is the truth.**

---

for journaling, i leave u with one question . . .

tell me, o magnificent one, what greatness awaits you?
for with love, all things are possible
know this

---

you do not need any*thing* or any*one* to be wildly alive.
you only need your connection to you
and with it, a new life begins . . .
yours.

(a.k.a. bring on da noise, bring on da funk, baby!)

turn me to where the sun rises,
so i can see the world's future.
turn me to where the sun sets,
so i can see the world's past.
stand me in the sun,
so i can hear the world's song of joy.

>> m. schroeder

>> one can never consent to creep when one feels an impulse to soar. <<
helen keller

b:
return to the very beginning, and get out the letter you wrote from you to your own soul
stating your intention. read it, and return it to its spot.
(you will look back upon it for years to come and smile at this memory.)

now, write a love letter from your soul to you — including any information / answers to your questions
or anything else it needs to say <> any guidance or inspiration it wishes to offer you. place it in your
sacred space and read as needed.

for infinite journaling: begin an inquiry of this question that will deepen and evolve as your self-connection
deepens . . . **what do i desire to give from my soul to the world? . . . to create, experience, and express
in this life?** these are the magic questions to keep asking for the rest of your life. remember:
as you receive, so, too, shall you give. soulfire is meant to awaken your ability to receive the gifts
of your own soul so that you are open and free to give them to the world.
and the world is forever changed because of it.

living your soul is like playing the game hot potato. once you have received your gifts, you must turn
around and give them to another. if you try to hide them or hold onto them, your fingers will start to
burn. know that your gifts require expression and action taken on their behalf. remember: pain is the
great messenger. when you feel it, it is always to tell you that you have more gifts to give this world. so
give them. every day. in every way that you can. in ways big and small = life orgasms big and small.

the power-of-you is this: as you awaken to and live your own soul, you awaken others to the fact that this
possibility even exists (as most of the world has no freakin idea it is even on the menu of life as a choice
and therefore repetitively dines instead on the not-so-happy meal of being disconnected). *until now.*
you, my friend, are the domino in the domino effect. hence: the individual and collective power of
self-connection. the personal becomes political by the very nature of the impact of your life upon the
whole. dang, it is good to be you.

my soul is awakened, my spirit is soaring.   >> anne brontë

c:

road map for your soul = keep your eye on the prize

lastly, from all of the things you have discovered through this process, set aside one evening (with the phone off) to do this very important assignment that is the culmination of this journey.

celebration:

throw yourself a coming out *partay* for your soul.

make your <u>own</u> soulfire soundtrack of the songs that really tell it, and then let it play . . . light candles and pour some champagne if u like. and please, put on your party shoes.

~ this is something to truly celebrate like nothing else you ever have or will ~

get a piece of foam board or easel, and go to town cutting out pictures, painting colors, writing words and statements that all sing the song of your soul and reflect what it is here to give, receive, experience, express, and create in your one precious life!

now materialize into form a collage, painting, poem, sculpture, or mural (or anything at all that calls out to you "make me! make me!"). create it as your commemoration of this journey and as a celebration of your own sacred soul and life!!!

keep it somewhere you can see everyday . . . and let it inspire you to daily action.

>> a plant can't live without roots. your soul is your root. <<
yogi bhajan

this reminder . . . this fire of your soul will allways lead you home into the beauty that is you and who you are here to become. just follow your roadmap . . . and then . . . *get ready to fly.*

---

trust your soul. it is who you are.+ never ever forget . . .

the world needs and is waiting for what you came to give.

---

be inspired by your own soulfire . . .

now, get out there and go live a revolution of love. (i will be looking for u.)

the most powerful weapon on earth is the human soul on fire.

>> field marshal ferdinand foch

amen.

soulfire

afterglow

a book must be

an ice-ax

to break up

the sea frozen

inside us.

>> franz kafka

thank you for taking this journey with me.

in truth, unity, and pure love,
(and, of course, with w-i-l-d soulfire)

brigitte secard
~ she who has a fiery passion for human possibility ~

you, your best thing. >> toni morrison, *beloved,* page 273

>> a writer is dear and necessary for us only in the measure of which they reveal to us the inner workings of their very soul. <<
leo tolstoy

soulfire starter creed

my life is an inspired celebration of the fire and purpose of my soul.
i live self-truth.

everyday of my life, i discover new ways to give and receive more love.

my accountability to my own soul sets the precedent for my real-ationship to the world and to all in it.
i follow the greatest leader and the only guru there is = my own soul.

gratitude, grace, and joy surround me. i seek to be contagious.

i breathe deeply and slowly. my grounded state gives me roots and wings.
i am fiercely unshakeable.

i am the power of compassion. i am the power of love. i am the power of truth.

the journey of my soul is **an adventure into aliveness** and bliss
and profound depths of love . . . and i have life orgasms pretty darn regularly.

i honor my body and sexuality. i am the power of creation.
+ to be a womanist, or to love one, is to rock the world with beauty and power.

i live a life of abundance and service. i am always sent what i need when i need it.

i am enslaved by no one and nothing, including myself. i realize *the personal is the political*
and that the expression of my own soul affects humanity deeply. i know that "the state of the union"
exists first in my own self. unity begins with one.

i am free . . . i am allways faithfull. i trust = i am at peace. i recognize the perfection and divine order in all things. i honor my past, exalt in my present, and smile at my future.

my heart is the messenger of my soul. my heart is the home of all truth. all of my emotions are sacred, and i take full ownership of them.

i am connected to all of creation. my eyes are open to the world as my own reflection. i practice humanity everywhere i go = i walk in equality.

there is nothing and no one more powerful than my own soul. here are the answers and meaning for all things. no one can ever give this or take this away from me.

i believe in the beauty of my soul. i am here for this. this is the gift i have been given in the miracle of my own existence . . . and it is the gift i humbly give back to the world.

my life is a revolution of love and of unity in action.

i embody, as a soulfire starter, a new possibility for the human condition.

x . . . .   date . . . .   let the joy begin.

___

self-authority + self-compassion + self-fire = wild aliveness
___

soulfire
for more information: inquire within

mission:
to inspire and celebrate the power and beauty of the human spirit
as it lives within your own soul . . .
and as it lives within the soul of every human being on the planet.

www.selftruth.com

about brigitte

as the original soulfire starter, brigitte secard is quite used to breaking the formula wherever she goes. at age 18, on fire about sexism yet decidedly not a feminist, she began training as a boxer. while fighting the power . . . she found it instead and blazed a new path for women: that of a womanist. to continue to study the concept of cultural and individual power, she put herself through college by doing singing telegrams so she could study political science. in her early 20s and on fire about racism and political inequality + with a fierce talent as a vocalist, she began to pursue a music career. offered several major recording contracts, she turned them all down after being told repeatedly by label execs: "just look good and sell records. no one cares about the truth." but she did care, so she recorded an independent album and then retired from the music industry. in her mid-20s with a fire that was beginning to burn as an inferno, she began to volunteer and study with gurus and spiritual masters of all kinds in order to deepen her understanding of leadership. what she found instead was a study in spiritual co-dependency: groups of people either up on a pedestal or bowed down before them all looking to each other for their liberation and no one looking in the only place it could be found: their own soul. she left these places and created a path that was at once both spiritual and political and that had never before been seen: one of self-truth and soul-authority with global impact. she began to work with people young and old, men and women, and people of all religions and backgrounds. it was at this point that the inferno of love ignited. at age 28, the book *soulfire* was written, and all of the pieces came together: womanist + love souldier + singer + entertainer + leader + self-truth innovator = a wildly alive revolutionary come to set the world **on fire.**
and she is doing just that.
let the joy begin.

brigitte now resides in west hollywood, california where she spreads love and starts soulfires everywhere she goes. even at the grocery store.

the end.

We hope this Jodere Group book has benefited you in your quest for personal, intellectual, and spiritual growth.

Jodere Group is passionate about bringing new and exciting books, such as *soulfire,* to readers worldwide. Our company was created as a unique publishing and multimedia avenue for individuals whose mission it is to impact the lives of others positively. We recognize the strength of an original thought, a kind word, and a selfless act — and the power of the individuals who possess them. We are committed to providing the support, passion, and creativity necessary for these individuals to achieve their goals and dreams.

Jodere Group is comprised of a dedicated and creative group of people who strive to provide the highest quality of books, audio programs, online services, and live events to people who pursue life-long learning. It is our personal and professional commitment to embrace our authors, speakers, and readers with helpfulness, respect, and enthusiasm.

For more information about our products, authors, or live events, please call 800.569.1002 or visit us on the Web at www.jodere.com.

JODERE
GROUP